I Believe in God

A Reflection on
the Apostles' Creed

Thomas P. Rausch, SJ

A Michael Glazier Book

LITURGICAL PRESS
Collegeville, Minnesota

www.litpress.org

A Michael Glazier Book published by Liturgical Press.

Cover design by Ann Blattner. Cover art: *The River* © 1987 by John August Swanson, serigraph, 30" x 19½", www.JohnAugustSwanson.com. Used with permission.

1   2   3   4   5   6   7   8

Library of Congress Cataloging-in-Publication Data
Rausch, Thomas P.
    I believe in God : a reflection on the Apostles' Creed /
Thomas P. Rausch.
        p.   cm.
    "A Michael Glazier book."
    Includes index.
    ISBN 978-0-8146-5260-2
    1. Apostles' Creed.   I. Title.

BT993.3.R38   2008
238'.11—dc22

2007030528

Professor Robert Earl Cushman
Duke University
In memoriam

Contents

The Holy Spirit

Acknowledgments

A book on the Apostles' Creed, the Christian community's baptismal confession of faith, is scarcely original. Scholars and pastors have written commentaries on the Creed in every age of the church's life. Martin Luther used the Apostles' Creed for the structure of his catechism. Joseph Ratzinger, now Pope Benedict XVI, used it as a framework for his enormously successful *Introduction to Christianity*, appearing now in at least seventeen different languages. Written shortly after the close of the Second Vatican Council, in light of what he saw as the proliferation of new or "modern" theologies, Ratzinger was concerned to "understand faith afresh" in a culture he described as at least still nominally Christian.[1]

Berard Marthaler used the Apostles' Creed and the longer Nicene-Constantinopolitan Creed for a comprehensive treatment of Catholic faith and life.[2] Nicholas Lash, in a brief commentary on the Apostles' Creed, analyzed it in the context of the mystery of the Trinity.[3] Luke Timothy Johnson has sought to make the Creed intelligible for those Christians who no longer understand or simply reject it; his book is particularly rich in setting the Creed against the background of Scripture.[4] While I have drawn occasionally on their works, the interpretation

---

[1] Joseph Ratzinger, *Introduction to Christianity* (San Francisco: Ignatius Press, 2004 [1968]) 32, citing the preface to the 1968 edition.

[2] Berard Marthaler, *The Creed: The Apostolic Faith in Contemporary Theology* (Mystic, CT: Twenty-Third Publications, 1993) vi.

[3] Nicholas Lash, *Believing Three Ways in One God: A Reading of the Apostles' Creed* (Notre Dame/London: University of Notre Dame Press, 1993).

[4] Luke Timothy Johnson, *The Creed: What Christians Believe and Why It Matters* (New York: Doubleday, 2003).

here is my own, done in a distinctly American context for an often polarized church.

I am grateful to old friend and colleague Michael Downey who read the manuscript and offered many helpful suggestions. I would also like to thank Susan Sink of Liturgical Press for her careful copyediting and our graduate assistant, Richard Garcia, for his help with proofreading. Special thanks to California artist John August Swanson for permission to use his serigraph, "The River," suggestive of the living waters in which we are immersed by baptism, for the cover.

Thomas P. Rausch, SJ

Abbreviations

Documents of Vatican II

DH	*Dignitatis humanae*: Declaration on Religious Freedom
DV	*Dei verbum*: Dogmatic Constitution on Divine Revelation
GS	*Gaudium et spes*: Pastoral Constitution on the Church in the Modern World
LG	*Lumen gentium*: Dogmatic Constitution on the Church
NA	*Nostra aetate*: Declaration on the Relationship of the Church to Non-Christian Religions
SC	*Sacrosanctum concilium*: Constitution on the Sacred Liturgy
UR	*Unitatis redintegratio*: Decree on Ecumenism

Other

CDF	Congregation for the Doctrine of the Faith
DS	Denzinger-Schönmetzer, *Enchiridion Symbolorum* 33rd ed. (Freiburg: Herder, 1965)
NAB	*New American Bible*

Introduction

What do we believe as Christians, and where can we find an authoritative summary of our faith? When I ask my students to name three or four basic Christian beliefs, their replies tend to be all over the field, many of them very subjective. Very few of them ever turn to the Creed.

Most religious communities express their faith in confessional statements or creeds (from the Latin *credo*, "I entrust," "I believe"). The great Jewish confession of faith, the *Shema* (the word means "to hear"), said on rising and retiring, proclaims, "Hear, O Israel! The Lord is our God, the Lord alone" (Deut 6:4). The *Shahaada*, the Muslim confession of faith, is recited numerous times throughout the day by devout Muslims in their prayer. It confesses, "I bear witness that there is no God but God, and I bear witness that Muhammad is the Messenger of God."

The faith of the Christian community is also summarized in creeds, most notably in what has been called since the fifth century the "Apostles' Creed" (*Symbolum Apostolicum*), as well as in the Nicene-Constantinopolitan Creed. The Apostles' Creed originated in the West, The Nicene-Constantinopolitan Creed developed from the great councils in the East. The Greek term *symbolum*, symbol or sign, means in this context a confession of faith. By the third century, it was being used for the baptismal interrogatories, the questions asked those to be baptized, and then for declaratory creeds.[1]

There are already various creeds or creedal statements in the New Testament, some of which were used in the baptismal rites of the early Christian communities.[2] Perhaps one of the earliest appears in 1 Corinthians,

---

[1] J. N. D. Kelly, *Early Christian Creeds* (New York: Longman, 1972).
[2] Kelly, *Early Christian Creeds*, 13.

where Paul says that no one can say "Jesus is Lord" except by the Holy Spirit (1 Cor 12:3). Another appears in Romans: "if you confess with your mouth that Jesus is Lord and believe in your heart that God raised him from the dead, you will be saved" (Rom 10:9; cf. 1 John 2:22; Rom 1:3-4). The setting for many of these primitive creeds was the church's worship, particularly its baptismal liturgies. Very influential was the baptismal formula that appears at the end of Matthew's Gospel, instructing the apostles to baptize "in the name of the Father, and of the Son, and of the holy Spirit" (Matt 28:19). The trinitarian structure of this formula most probably shaped the structure of the later creeds of the church.

Reviewing early authors such as Irenaeus, Tertullian, and Hippolytus, Jaroslav Pelikan finds two elements that remain constant in their different creedal phrases: "one or both of them may safely be said to have formed the outline of most creeds." One element uses the trinitarian language of Father, Son, and Holy Spirit, the other refers to the life, death, and resurrection of Jesus Christ.[3] The language of Father, Son, and Holy Spirit reflects the trinitarian structure that is basic to the creeds, for Christian life is a communion in God's triune life.

The Apostles' Creed

Behind the Apostles' Creed lies the early interrogatory baptismal creed of the Roman church, dated from the end of the second century. The earliest version of it appears in Hippolytus' *Apostolic Tradition* (21.12-18), a text from approximately 215 CE. Those to be baptized were asked three questions, enabling them to profess their belief in God as Father, Son, and Spirit before each immersion in the baptismal waters.

> Do you believe in God the Father Almighty?
>
> Do you believe in Christ Jesus, the Son of God, Who was born by the Holy Spirit from the Virgin Mary, who was crucified under Pontius Pilate, and died, and rose again on the third day living from the dead, and ascended into the heavens, and sat down on the right hand of the Father, and will come to judge the living and the dead?
>
> Do you believe in the Holy Spirit, in the holy church and in the resurrection of the body?

---

[3] Jaroslav Pelikan, *The Emergence of the Catholic Tradition (100–600)* (Chicago: University of Chicago Press, 1971) 117.

As Joseph Ratzinger, now Pope Benedict XVI, has noted, this baptismal formula was both confession of faith and part of the actual sacrament; thus the Creed has real meaning only as a verbal expression of the act of conversion.[4] In other words, baptism was not mere ritual, as it so often is today, but the graced response of someone who had undergone a profound conversion to faith in the triune God, and now confessed it publicly as he or she was sacramentally initiated into the community of the church. Similarly, to say the Latin *"credo"* in the context of the liturgy is more than the expression of an opinion about God's existence. It is a "performative" utterance, that is, a pledge or promise "that life and love, mind, heart, and all my actions, are set henceforward steadfastly on God, and God alone."[5]

The present Apostles' Creed is what J. N. D. Kelly calls "a rather elaborate variant" of the Old Roman Creed which goes back to at least the first half of the fourth century.[6] With minor differences, we have examples of it in Latin from Rufinus (404), and in Greek from Marcellus (340). It was Rufinus who passed on the story that the Creed was composed by the apostles, leading subsequent commentators to attempt to find in it twelve articles of faith, each supposedly composed by an apostle. Even if the story is more legend than fact, it remains true that the Christian faith summarized in the Creed finds its origin in the apostolic tradition transmitted from the beginning by the church. The title "Apostles' Creed" (*symbolum apostolorum*) is first seen in a letter sent by the Synod of Milan (390) to Pope Siricius. At this same time the Creed was being described as "the rule of faith," the standard of what was to be believed. The *Catechism of the Catholic Church* calls the Apostles' Creed "the oldest Roman catechism" (no. 196).

From Martin Luther comes the tradition of describing the Creed in terms of three articles, belief in God the Father, belief in Jesus Christ his only Son, and belief in the Holy Spirit. This provided the structure for Luther's catechism and will provide the structure for our study also.

---

[4] Joseph Ratzinger, *Principles of Catholic Theology: Building Stones for a Fundamental Theology* (San Francisco: Ignatius Press, 1987) 34–35.

[5] Nicholas Lash, *Believing Three Ways in One God: A Reading of the Apostles' Creed* (Notre Dame/London: University of Notre Dame Press, 1993) 18. Perhaps a sense for this performative dimension of the creed lies behind Rome's insistence that *credo* be translated "I believe," rather than the "we believe" that has been common since Vatican II.

[6] Kelly, *Early Christian Creeds*, 369.

While the New Testament is rich in a variety of theologies, the great utility of the Apostles' Creed is that it presents the Christian faith as a single story, what the New Testament and the fathers of the church often referred to as God's *oikonomia* (Greek = economy, or plan) (cf. Eph 1:10).[7]

In more contemporary language, we might describe it as a brief statement of the Christian "metanarrative." Beginning with God and God's work as creator, its central drama includes the incarnation, death, and resurrection of Jesus, our involvement in the Spirit through the church, and our final destiny. Pope Benedict has called the Creed "a tiny *summa* in which everything essential is expressed."[8] It is the "rule of faith," not simply theology or a particular interpretation of faith, but a confession of what Christians believe.

When needed we will draw on the more developed Creed of Nicaea (325) and Constantinople (381), known formally as the Nicene-Constantinopolitan Creed or sometimes as the Ecumenical Creed. From the sixth century on it has been recited or sung as part of the liturgy.

The Present Approach

If the Creed is ancient, the context for this book is contemporary; it offers a reflection on the Creed in a pluralistic American context for those in an often polarized church. Some Catholics today are reformists. They question Catholicism's institutional structures, minimize its uniqueness, struggle with what they see as its patriarchal language, and reduce traditional beliefs such as the virgin birth and the resurrection of the body to mere symbols. Some, influenced by a postmodern "culture of choice" in which spirituality has been divorced from religion, construct their own religious identities without reference to Scripture, tradition, or church. Others are more traditional. Uncomfortable with evolution, they advocate the incorporation of theories of "creation science" or "intelligent design" into school curricula or object to a less literal approach to many of the biblical narratives. Their individualistic understanding of salvation is at times scarcely distinguishable from that of fundamentalist Protestantism.

Since the story of God's entering into relationship with humankind is at the heart of the Apostles' Creed, we will have to pay special attention

---

[7] See *Catechism of the Catholic Church*, no. 236.

[8] "What is the Creed?" *Origins* 36, no. 16 (2006) 258.

to Scripture. This means taking the biblical witness seriously. Too often modern theology has moved beyond Scripture as the inspired witness to God's revelation in the books of the Old and New Testament and particularly in the person of Jesus of Nazareth. Scripture cannot be reduced to mere history, reflected in the text or lying behind it, as though it was merely a historical document. Nor can it be dismissed as simply the literary traditions of ancient peoples and communities. It is, as Sandra Schneiders argues, a revelatory text.[9]

At the same time, Scripture cannot be reduced to a number of isolated texts collected to "prove" some position that is more confessional than truly biblical or simply the opinion of a particular preacher. Taking the biblical text seriously means respecting the theologies that emerge from Paul, Luke, or John, and interpreting them in their full integrity. It means that the Scripture is interpreted in the context of the apostolic tradition of the church that received it, particularly as that tradition comes to expression in the fathers of the church, the creeds, the sacraments, and the liturgy. This is how Pope Benedict approaches Scripture. His reverence for the word of God as something constitutive of the church and Christian life makes him stand out from many theologians today, both Catholic and Protestant. "Scripture alone," he writes, "is theology in the fullest sense of the word because it truly has God as its subject; it does not just speak of him, but *is* his own speech. It lets God himself speak."[10]

Because of the pluralism that exists even within the Catholic Church, we will begin our reflection on the Creed with a Prolegomenon, a preliminary discussion to set the context for what follows. Chapter One will consider two traditional approaches to the question of God, one through reason, the other through revelation. Chapter Two will consider the nature of theological language in which God's revelation in Christ is expressed. The three articles of the Apostles' Creed will provide the basic structure for the book, Part One, belief in God the Father; Part Two, belief in Jesus Christ, God's only Son; and Part Three, belief in the Holy Spirit.

Thus this book will attempt to "unpack" the three articles of the Creed. We will approach them as a fundamental statement of the faith to which each Christian is committed by baptism. We will attempt to show how these articles developed out of the biblical tradition, came to

---

[9] Sandra M. Schneiders, *The Revelatory Text: Interpreting the New Testament as Sacred Scripture* (Collegeville, MN: Liturgical Press, 1999) 22–23.

[10] Ratzinger, *Principles of Catholic Theology*, 321.

expression in the church's liturgy and creeds, and are understood today in light of contemporary theological reflection. We will also try to understand how this language makes sense in terms of our experience.

The mystery of the Trinity is at the heart of the faith into which we were baptized. A particular concern will be to explore the basic Christian conviction that God's self-disclosure as Father, Son, and Spirit gives us a share in the divine life and thus brings us into communion with one another. Always the concern is the God who calls us into relationship, the God whose very nature is to be in relation. At the end we will consider again the personal nature of God, the triune God who we come to experience as Father, Son, and Spirit.

Prolegomenon

Chapter 1

Reason and Revelation

Is there a God? How do we know if God exists? What is the nature of the divine? Is God gracious towards us? These questions of belief and unbelief are timeless, no less important today than at any time in the past, though perhaps more difficult to answer in a skeptical, postmodern culture that so often reduces truth to personal opinion. In a culture of unbelief, what lies behind our creedal declaration: "I believe in God"?

For many people the existence of God is self-evident. They sense God's presence in the beauty of the natural world and the divine intelligence in the things that are made, what the psalmist calls the works of God's hands (cf. Ps 8:6; 92:5). Such people cannot believe that the intricacies of the sub-microphysical world or the majesty of the stars and planets are the result of chance, any more than I could believe that the computer on which I'm working assembled itself from bits of carbon, silicon, and sand. For others, God speaks in silence, in the whisper of the breeze or the good clean smell of the earth. Their personal response to these intimations of the divine presence is awe before the mystery.

But there are many who are not able to believe. There is too much evil and tragedy, too many victims of injustice, too many broken hearts for them to believe in an intelligent and merciful God. Some argue that modern science has made belief in God an unnecessary hypothesis. Humankind has come of age; it is now able to live without the comforting myths and superstitions of an earlier era. The very word "modernity," rooted in the spirit of the Enlightenment, seems to rule out belief in a divine presence, while the ethos known as postmodernism questions even the possibility of objective truth.

Perhaps the easiest believers to identify in today's world are Muslims. I've seen Muslim men in airport lounges, kneeling in prayer facing Mecca. Or Muslim women in head scarves among the young women in tank tops and low-cut jeans on our campuses. Islam may well be the dominant faith in a few decades, at least in Europe. There are already predictions that some European countries, given their very low birthrates, could have Muslim majorities by the end of the century.

The sad fact is that many who were raised as Christians are no longer able to assent to the Creed. They are not believers, or at least do not visibly practice their faith. And many have questions. Is religion simply a creation of the human longing for meaning and an absolute in a world of shifting values and changeable certainties? How do we know that our ideas of God are not simply the projections of our own desires or hopes? How do we know that we are not bowing before an idol of our own creation? Can we disentangle subjectivity and religious sentimentality from the mystery of the divine, the holy, which is both terrifying and fascinating?[1] Thus the fundamental question, how can we know or encounter this divine mystery? Has God addressed a word to humankind?

Twenty-five hundred years ago Plato raised this question in the *Phaedo*, his dialogue on the death of his friend, Socrates. As Socrates sought to reassure his disciples about his belief in the soul's immortality, Plato through his character Simmias acknowledges the difficulty of attaining to any real certainty in the present life, short of finding "some word of God which will more surely and safely carry him."[2] While the context is different here, the question Plato raised is the same, and it is fundamental. Has there been a revelation, a word from God, some self-disclosure of the divine mystery?

Christian Apologetics

Since the first days of the church, Christian apologists have sought to answer this question in the affirmative, showing how God has spoken to us in the words of Holy Scripture and definitively in the person of Jesus. Apologetics has always involved giving reasons for faith; thus it is an effort to bring faith and reason into harmony. In his *History of Apologetics*, Cardinal Avery Dulles points out that while its goals and methods have shifted over the centuries, apologetics has always been concerned

---

[1] Rudolf Otto, *The Idea of the Holy* (New York: Oxford University Press, 1958).

[2] *Phaedo*, Harvard Classics, available in many online editions, trans. Benjamin Jowett, par. 370.

with the dialogue between the believer and the unbeliever, even the unbeliever that rests within the apologist's own heart.[3]

Classical apologetics generally proceeds in two stages. First, it seeks to establish the existence of God on the basis of reason, a philosophical approach, called natural theology, which became especially important in the early modern period. Then it argues that revelation is at least possible, that the gospels accurately witness to God's revelation in Jesus and help us know him as teacher and Lord. Sometimes Catholics have added a third *demonstratio catholica*, to address the particular claims of the Catholic Church.

Natural Theology

Natural theology traditionally offers various philosophical arguments for the existence of God based on the existence, motion, order, design, and perfection of the natural world. Thomas Aquinas, a thirteenth-century Dominican theologian and doctor of the church, summarized these arguments in his famous "five ways."[4] The first argument, from motion, comes from Aristotle, who looked to an unmoved mover or God (*ho theos*), who alone could explain the motion of the world. Since nothing can move unless put in motion by another, to avoid an infinite regress there must be an unmoved first mover. The second argument is from efficient causality. Since no thing can cause itself, which would require that it exist prior to itself, there must be an uncaused first cause.

The third argument, perhaps Aquinas' most profound insight, is from possibility or necessity, often called the argument from contingency. Aquinas reasoned that things in nature are observed to be generated and corrupted, and thus are possible to be and not to be. But it is impossible for these things always to be, since that which is possible not to be at some time is not. Now if everything could not be, that is, if everything is contingent, dependent for its existence on something else, then at one time there could have been nothing in existence, and there would be nothing even now. His conclusion is that there must be one thing whose existence is necessary, to avoid another infinite regress. Thus he postulates the existence of a being whose *nature* is to be, a necessary being which does not receive existence, like contingent beings, but gives it to others.

[3] Avery Dulles, *A History of Apologetics* (second edition) (San Francisco: Ignatius Press, 2005) xx.

[4] Thomas Aquinas, *Summa Theologica*, trans. by the Fathers of the English Dominican Province, I,2,3.

The fourth argument is from the gradations found in things. It proceeds from gradations of perfections to their full realization. The cause of the perfection in any genus must be something which itself has the perfection of being, goodness, or beauty, which we call God.

The fifth or final argument is from the governance of the world, often called the argument from teleology. All things, including those that lack intelligence, act for some desired end. Just as the arrow needs to be directed towards its target by the archer, so natural things are directed by some intelligent being which we call God.

Aquinas' *Quinque Via,* or Five Ways, summarize the arguments from motion, efficient cause, contingency, perfection, and design. They are not "proofs" in the sense that they are not demonstrations for those who do not accept the premises. Thus they don't work for all. For others, however, they offer sufficient evidence or reason to affirm the existence of God, although they are far from telling us *who* God is. But affirming God's existence also affirms the possibility of a being that might bridge the chasm between itself and contingent beings like ourselves in the world of experience, thus, the possibility of a divine revelation.

In his famous autobiography, *The Seven Storey Mountain,* Thomas Merton describes how his own encounter with Aquinas' argument from contingency was to revolutionize his life. Born in France of parents who were artists, Merton had grown up an agnostic without any real religious faith. Hitherto he had seen the God of Christians largely as a projection of their own superstitions, desires, and ideals, an impossible being combining all the emotions of which humans are capable. How could one believe in such a God? But when he began reading Etienne Gilson's book, *The Spirit of Medieval Philosophy,* he found himself for the first time confronted with Aquinas' idea of a God who was pure act, whose very nature was to exist. Gilson used the word "aseity" to describe this unique way of existing, in virtue of its own nature, by itself (Latin: *a se*), without cause.

In other words, unlike all other beings which are beings only by participation, God is pure Being. In God, essence and existence are the same. Merton wrote, "here was a notion of God that was at the same time deep, precise, simple and accurate and, what is more, charged with implications which I could not even begin to appreciate."[5] Suddenly the possibility of Christian faith opened up for him.

---

[5] Thomas Merton, *The Seven Storey Mountain* (New York: Harcourt Brace Jovanovich, 1976 [first published 1948]) 172; Gilson's work that so influenced Merton was *The Spirit of Medieval Philosophy* (New York: Charles Scribner's Sons, 1940).

Revelation

Christianity presupposes that God has bridged the chasm between the creature and the creator, or in more secular terms, between the human longing for something ultimate and the mystery of being itself, bringing the two into relationship. But without minimizing in any way the divine initiative, revelation comes in and through our ordinary experience. It is mediated through popular stories, historical crises, prophetic insight, and the wisdom of sages.

The term revelation (Greek: *apocalypsis*, "the lifting of the veil") refers to God's uncovering or self-communication to human beings. But revelation does not come to us in neatly formulated truths, whether in sacred Scripture or magisterial pronouncements, as a propositional model of revelation would suggest.[6] In its Dogmatic Constitution on Divine Revelation (*Dei verbum*), the Second Vatican Council speaks of God's revelation being realized through God's action in the history of Israel and its interpretation through the prophetic word, reaching its fulfillment in the life, death, and resurrection of Jesus, the Word made flesh (DV 1–4).

Thus Christian revelation is not primarily verbal (as Islam teaches) or propositional (as many fundamentalist Christians think), but personal. Unlike evangelical Protestants, Catholics do not claim an absolute inerrancy for Scripture. Vatican II taught that "we must acknowledge that the books of scripture, firmly, faithfully and without error, teach that truth which God, for the sake of our salvation, wished to see confided to the sacred scriptures" (DV 11).

Rooted in Experience

Revelation originates always in experience, whether in the stories and traditions of the people of the first covenant or in the experience of the disciples of Jesus. Israel's sacred writings, a mix of history remembered, retold, and reinterpreted in light of present events, represents a multifaceted account of their relationship with their God. Called by Christians the Old Testament, these books in summary tell the story of a Semitic people, diverse in origin, who in the thirteenth century BCE migrated out of an oppressive Egypt and ultimately into the land of Canaan under the leadership of a charismatic figure named Moses. After years of struggle to establish themselves in the land, the various tribes,

[6] See Avery Dulles, *Models of Revelation* (Garden City, NY: Doubleday, 1983).

traditionally twelve, were united by David who chose as his capital the ancient city of Jerusalem. When the unity forged under David collapsed in later generations and they lost their independence because of foreign conquest and went into exile, they began to look forward to a new intervention of God on their behalf, though by the first century BCE there were many diverse expressions of this hope.

Christianity has its origin in the figure of Jesus of Nazareth, a Jew who lived in the first three decades of the Common Era (CE). Jesus began a movement that preached to his contemporaries, many of them poor, gathered a group of disciples, and had at their center a symbolic group known as "the Twelve," representative of a renewed or eschatological Israel. His teaching centered on the "reign of God" being at hand. He cannot be understood simply as a reforming rabbi, mitigating the requirements of the Law, or as a political messiah, and he was far more than an ethical teacher. The reign of God he proclaimed was inseparable from his own person and ministry. Known as a miracle worker and healer, he was criticized for his teaching and for his association with those marginalized by the religious community. After a relatively brief ministry, he was put to death by representatives of the Jerusalem priesthood who conspired with the occupying Roman authorities, but his followers from the beginning claimed that God had restored him to life and continued to gather and teach in his name. The continuing assembly (Greek: *ekklesia*) of his followers down to our own day we call the church.

When we review the history of Israel and the earliest Christian community, it becomes evident that for the peoples of these communities, it is precisely in the events of their ordinary human lives, in encounters both mundane and extraordinary, in tragedy and hope and self-transcendence, in examples of love, compassion, and self-sacrifice, that God's grace becomes transparent and the divine self-disclosure takes place. As Edward Schillebeeckx argues, "revelation and experience are not opposites. God's revelation follows the course of human experiences."[7]

Symbolically Mediated

Experience, however, even the religious experience reflected in the Bible, is never pure. It is always embedded in feelings, insights, and images, in works of imagination and intelligence, in personal and historical

---

[7] Edward Schillebeeckx, *Interim Report on the Books Jesus and Christ* (New York: Crossroad, 1982) 11.

events. And it is mediated to others by language, story, and symbol. As the literary theorist Paul Ricoeur likes to say, symbol gives rise to thought.[8] Living in a prescientific culture, the Israelites' world was rich in legends, myths of origin, and folk epics. They cherished and embroidered the stories of their ancestors. Nor were they shy about borrowing from the cultural concepts, stories, and traditions of their neighbors.

Some of these stories they employed to describe their own experience of God. One of them was the Akkadian cosmogony known as *Enuma Elish*, the story of the Babylonian god Marduk's victory over Tiamat, the bloated female dragon who personified the watery chaos from which the earth was created. We can acknowledge that the creation accounts in Genesis are "mythic," in the sense that they are prescientific, but still teach profound truths about God and our human condition that are not accessible to rational or empirical investigation. We'll return to this in detail in the discussion of how we understand God as creator.

Similarly the Israelite authors adapted the popular Mesopotamian story of the great flood, the *Epic of Gilgamesh*. An early Sumerian version dates from the third millennium BCE. As in the Genesis story, when the gods decree a deluge, the hero Utnapishtim is ordered to build a great rectangular ship or ark onto which he leads "the beasts of the field, the wild creatures of the field." After seven days and nights of rain the storm ends, the waters subside, and all humankind "had returned to clay." As the ship grounds itself on a mountain, Utnapishtim sets free first a dove, then a swallow, and finally a raven which finds a place to rest, after which he offers up a sacrifice.[9] Those familiar with the Genesis account will recognize that the *Epic of Gilgamesh* is basically the same story, but with a very different theology.

The Old Testament is full of such stories, and they are rich in meaning, though their meaning is often religious rather than historical. The story of the fall in Genesis 3 is an attempt to explain how God's creation, which from the beginning was good, was tainted by the evil introduced by humans in their desire to be like God. In Gerhard von Rad's marvelous reconstruction of the theology of the Hexateuch (the first six books of the Bible), humankind's violation of the divine order, beginning with the disobedience of Adam and Eve, lets back into creation with devastating

[8] Paul Ricoeur, *The Conflict of Interpretations*, ed. Don Ihde (Evanston, IL: Northwestern University Press, 1974) 288.

[9] See James B. Pritchard, ed. *The Ancient Near East: An Anthology of Texts and Pictures* (Princeton University Press, 1958) 68–69.

effect the watery chaos which God overcame in the first creation story, until God must intervene to save creation in the story of the great flood.[10] In other words, sin affects not just human beings, but creation itself.

Some stories have practical intent. The story of the sons of Noah, one of whom was Ham, the father of Canaan, who violates his father's honor by gazing on him in his nakedness (Gen 9:20-27) is included to show God's displeasure with the Canaanites whose fertility cult involving ritual prostitution was a constant threat to the religion of Israel. The political concept of covenant, a ritual agreement between peoples and city states, was used to express Yahweh's special relationship with Israel. The great story of the Exodus from Egypt, a story both of liberation and the creation of a people, becomes a symbol of God's saving work. It was told over and over again and celebrated ritually in the Passover Supper (Exod 12); in subsequent generations it was used to interpret later Israelite experience.

As Israel struggled with national failure, the humiliation of exile, and collective guilt, various traditions developed which looked for and imagined a future deliverance. Brueggemann shows how such imaginative preaching can mediate new ways of perceiving, experiencing, and believing, and thus a new world, a process he notes was once called conversion.[11] During Israel's Babylonian captivity, for example, the prophet known as Second Isaiah assured the people of God's faithfulness (Isa 49:15-16; 54:10). "The exile was widely seen to be a season of God's absence, and now this poet dares to assert that God is present in that very circumstance, faithfully at work to bring a newness out of the defeat."[12]

Thus the messianic tradition, looking forward to a new intervention of God in the life of the people, developed from the preaching of the prophets from the eighth century down to the end of the exile. The Wisdom tradition, with its roots in both the home and the school attached to the Jerusalem court, continues down to the very late Book of Wisdom, the last book in the Old Testament, composed in the last half of the first century BCE. Wisdom was concerned with a theology of creation, the mystery of suffering, and personal morality. Apocalyptic

---

[10] Gerhard von Rad, *Old Testament Theology: Volume I: The Theology of Israel's Historical Traditions* (New York: Harper and Row, 1962) 154–58.

[11] Walter Brueggemann, *Cadences of Home: Preaching Among Exiles* (Louisville, KY: Westminster John Knox Press, 1997) 32–35.

[12] Ibid., 19.

literature, developing from 200 BCE to 100 CE, looked forward to the end of the present order, even of the world itself, and the inauguration of a new age. It represents a work of imagination, giving hope to a people whose way of life was under threat by envisioning an alternative future. As Jews were dying for their faith under the persecution of Antiochus IV (167–164 BCE), the idea of a life beyond death appears for the first time in the tradition, expressed by the image of the resurrection of the dead (Dan 12:1-3; 2 Mac 7:1-41; 14:46). Here a crisis in the life of the community leads to hope for Yahweh's raising the dead to life and a new symbol of the resurrection of the body, in other words, to a theology of hope.

Thus the Old Testament reflects a great variety of ancient Near-Eastern myths and legends, stories of creation and the loss of innocence, political concepts such as covenant, epic stories rooted in history like the great saga of the Exodus (originally a migration of peoples which became a metaphor for God's salvific action or salvation), court histories and legal codes, prophetic, wisdom, and apocalyptic literature, all rich in metaphor and symbol.

Conclusion

The *Catechism of the Catholic Church* affirms that the "existence of God the Creator can be known with certainty through his works, by the light of human reason, even if this knowledge is often obscured and disfigured by error. This is why faith comes to confirm and enlighten reason in the correct understanding of this truth."[13]

Not all are swayed by metaphysical arguments for the existence of God such as we have considered, or by historical appraisals of the tradition. Today a healthy skepticism has too often given way to a pervasive relativism, suspicious of all truth claims. There are only "truths," multiple and diverse. What has been lost is the very concept of truth itself, and the God on whose existence truth depends. This postmodernist ethos, with its skepticism and relativism, dominates the academic culture of the contemporary university and shapes the world in which we live.

How do those who suspect that there is something more than the secular, postmodernist worldview admits resolve issues of faith and belief? Dean Hoge and his associates have described contemporary

---

[13] *Catechism of the Catholic Church*, no. 286.

American culture, with its religious individualism, as "the culture of choice." With so many people claiming to experience the sacred outside of religious institutions, with so many "seekers" and so much religious consumerism, spirituality has been uncoupled from religion and many people, particularly young adults, seem to construct their own religious identities on the basis of subjective feelings and personal preference.[14] Many speak of "a God I am comfortable with" or "my own personal faith" or "creating my own spirituality." They insist, "I'm spiritual but not religious."

In over thirty years of teaching, I repeatedly encounter students who say that they believe in God, but it is not a God of the Scriptures, the Christian tradition, or the teaching of the church. It is a God of their own conceiving. In a prescient essay entitled, "The Unbelief of Believers," Thomas Merton characterized modern unbelievers as completely uninterested in a God "who speaks or makes demands. . . . Their 'god' is simply an explanation and purification for the comfort and confusion of affluent society."[15]

However, many have been moved by what the French mathematician and philosopher Blaise Pascal (1623–1662) called "reasons of the heart." In his famous *Pensées* he argues that the heart has reasons which reason itself does not know (no. 277), for "it is the heart which experiences God, and not the reason" (no. 278).[16] Just as Augustine had written, "Our hearts are made for you Oh God, and they shall not rest until they rest in you,"[17] so Pascal appeals specifically to intuition (no. 288), that sense that there is something more, something mysterious but real. He points to the God who is disclosed in our hearts, the God we intuit, drawing us toward himself, the God known by the humble and the poor even without rational proof. But Pascal does not mean dismissing reason and relying on emotion or sentimentality.

Pascal's sense for the truth of Christianity, drawing those who open themselves to the Spirit's presence in their hearts, finding not proofs but reasons to believe in the Christian story, will be our approach here. Metaphysical arguments are more helpful for some than for others; they

---

[14] Dean Hoge and others, *Young Adult Catholics: Religion in the Culture of Choice* (Notre Dame, IN: University of Notre Dame Press, 2001) 15–16.

[15] Thomas Merton, *Faith and Violence: Christian Teaching and Christian Practice* (Notre Dame, IN: University of Notre Dame Press, 1968) 201.

[16] Blaise Pascal, *Pensée*, trans. W. F. Trotter, online edition.

[17] Augustine, *Confessions*, I, 1.

can serve as a *preparatio fidei* (a preparation for faith), making the case for the intelligibility of a God who might speak a revealing word.

Even more important is the biblical tradition which witnesses to God's self-disclosure in history. The Old Testament, when seen from a historical perspective, testifies to a growing expectation of some definitive intervention in the life of Israel. The New Testament confesses that God has come in the life, death, and resurrection of Jesus of Nazareth, the Jesus "who is himself both the mediator and the sum total of revelation" (DV 2).

Chapter 2

Theology and Its Language

When we recite the Creed, we affirm our faith in the truths that come to us through the church about God. Our relationship to God, indeed our salvation, is rooted in that faith, and our ability to affirm that faith as members of the community. Revelation begins in the experience of the religious community, but it is mediated by language, symbol, and story. In order to explore the Creed, we need to first look at the way we express our faith theologically. What is it we say about our experience and beliefs? What does it mean to say it in a particular, *theological* way? In this chapter we will consider the task of theology, the nature of theological language, and its expression in doctrine and theological traditions.

Theology

Telling a story to teach a religious lesson or retelling these stories or traditions in the light of new experience—the work of prophets and editors—is already to theologize. Gerhard von Rad states that "re-telling remains the most legitimate form of theological discourse on the Old Testament."[1] For example, while some references to creation in the Old Testament are quite old and reflect the creation theologies of Israel's neighbors, much of what we actually find in the Old Testament today

---

[1] Gerhard Von Rad, *Old Testament Theology*, Vol. 1 (New York: Harper and Row, 1962) 121.

reflects the work of later editors who linked creation with God's saving work in Israel's history. For the fifth-century BCE Priestly editors who gave us the first five books of the Bible in their present form, the Genesis story of creation was the beginning of that work. The prophet we call Second Isaiah, writing towards the end of the Exile, looked forward to a new Exodus, a return from exile and new future (Isa 43:16-21).[2] Similarly, for Walter Brueggemann, "Israel characteristically retold *all* of its experience through the powerful, definitional lens of the Exodus memory."[3]

The development of the New Testament tradition was similar. Since the earliest Christians were Jews, they reread their own religious tradition to find the language and theology to express the meaning of Jesus' life, ministry, and death. In their preaching and later written texts they used the figures, metaphors, and titles from the Old Testament as they proclaimed what God had done in Jesus. Jesus was prophet, messiah, and Lord, the Son of Man (the only title he seems to have used of himself), Son of David, and Son of God. He was the Word of God, the Wisdom of God, and sometimes simply God. All of this of course was language derived from the Jewish tradition.

The Nature of Theology

What then is theology? From the time of St. Anselm (d. 1109), theology has been understood as faith seeking understanding (Latin: *fides quaerens intellectum*). Anselm's definition, which places the emphasis on faith, helps us to grasp that theology is different from other kinds of knowing. Theology implies knowledge which is more personal than objective; it is based on a personal relationship which is intrinsic to faith. God is not an object, like other objects in the world that can be observed and studied. God is personal, a subject. Just as we never know another person completely, and only understand them as they disclose themselves to us, so we only partially understand the mystery of God. We come to know God in word and sacrament. Therefore, the object of theology is God's self-disclosure, mediated by a community of faith.

Theology is very different from religious studies or the philosophy of religion, "objective" studies which do not presume a personal faith commitment. Theology is the effort of the believer or more exactly the believing community to understand its faith, to bring to expression its ex-

---

[2] Ibid., 136–39.

[3] Walter Brueggemann, *Theology of the Old Testament: Testimony, Dispute, Advocacy* (Minneapolis: Fortress Press, 1997) 177.

perience of God. It is the effort to find the words, stories, analogies, metaphors, and language to express that faith experience and to reexpress it in light of further knowledge, deeper insights, and higher viewpoints. In this section we will look at both God's self-disclosure through revelation and the mediation of that revelation by the church.

In the words of Karl Rahner, theology is "the conscious and methodological explanation and explication of the divine revelation received and grasped in faith."[4] Thus theology can be termed the science of faith, for it is a properly scientific discipline with its own methods, procedures, and specialties. It can never be reduced to opinion. Nonetheless, God's revelation in Christ is mediated historically. Each theological discipline explores an aspect of God's revelation in Christ and its implications for God's people. Biblical theology reflects on God's revelation in Scripture and the person of Jesus; historical theology studies its transmission in the Christian tradition. Systematic theology is both constructive and critical; it seeks to understand and make intelligible the doctrines of faith and show how they are related to one another. Moral theology reflects on Christian life and discipleship, thus on questions of ethics, both personal and social. Pastoral theology is concerned with building up the Christian community through liturgy and preaching, spiritual formation, religious education, and service.

Secondly, even when done by individuals, Christian theology is properly a work of the church. God's revelation is mediated communally, first through the people of Israel, and then through the community of the church, with its Scripture, its sacraments, and its apostolic ministry. Catholic theology is done within the tradition of the church and its official teaching.[5] Thus as a science, theology has a critical dimension; it must be systematic in its pursuit of truth and open to what is known from other sciences or areas of knowledge. It helps the church to reflect critically on its language and proclamation, sometimes reformulating it or incorporating a higher viewpoint, precisely for the sake of the Gospel, and it challenges individuals to a deeper understanding and appropriation of the Christian mystery. Both individuals and the church itself can become complacent, resting comfortably in the familiar and the traditional, rather than being open to the Spirit's work in bringing both to

---

[4] Karl Rahner, "Theology," *Encyclopedia of Theology: The Concise Sacramentum Mundi*, ed. Karl Rahner (New York: Seabury Press, 1975) 1687.

[5] See Avery Dulles, "Criteria of Catholic Theology," *Communio* 22, no. 2 (1995) 304.

a deeper appreciation of God's truth that remains always beyond our own efforts to capture it in language and theology. A faith that is not questioned and refined through critical reflection can easily lapse into various forms of superstition, fundamentalism, or ideology.

At the same time, as a work of the church, theology must seek to be faithful to the church's tradition; it must stay in communion with the community of faith and its apostolic authority, remaining rooted in the experience of the community from which it developed. Otherwise it dissolves into an amorphous pluralism of competing theories and ideologies, losing its clarity and force like water poured out on sand.

Theological Language

If theology describes the effort of the believing community to understand its religious experience, to bring it to expression in stories, analogies, metaphors, and language, it will of necessity use a variety of languages, whether narrative, philosophical, or mythic. In this section we need to consider more carefully the nature of theological language.

Because theology often uses such imaginative language, much of its language is described as mythic or mythopoetic. The term myth, as it is used in theology, is a technical one; it does not mean something that is not true, but something that is true in a different sense than a literal reading would suggest. For example, the Genesis story of the Deluge is about the destructive power of sin, not an actual, historical event. We live by myths, that is to say, by the symbols, stories, and what postmodernists call "metanarratives," the archetypal stories that give meaning to our lives. The Christian metanarrative includes the story of the creation, fall, redemption, and final gathering of the saints.

Myths are different from historical narratives and scientific explanations; they express what is true from a religious or human perspective, even if it cannot be historically proved or scientifically established. Science and history have their own criteria of verifiability. But truth is so much greater than what can be empirically demonstrated. Thus myths help us bridge the gap between our direct experience and what remains mysterious. When thinking about this contemporary language of myth we should keep in mind that God's Spirit can inspire and teach through stories as well as through prophetic oracles or historical narratives.

Because "theology" means literally "words about God," a God who remains beyond our direct experience, there is a tentative quality to our theological language. It is largely an analogical language. Analogy grasps a similarity between two things, one familiar, the other more distant from our direct experience. We say that God is Father, rock, love, etc., to affirm something about the divine mystery from what is familiar to us. Catholic theology describes this analogy between God and created beings as the "analogy of being" (*analogia entis*). At the same time, we have to say that God is not like the fathers, rocks, and love we know from our ordinary experience; God is both less and much more. Thus Christian theology proceeds by a threefold declension, first the way of affirmation (the *via affirmativa*), then by negation (the *via negativa*), and finally by eminence, a way of assigning to God qualities known from ordinary experience that goes beyond our ability to comprehend.

The expression of a truth in doctrinal language, itself theological, is not always identical with the truth it affirms. All human expressions of divine truth, whether biblical narratives, theologies, or official teachings of the church, remain historically conditioned, limited by the expressive power of their language and by the limited knowledge, specific concerns, and conceptual categories of the time of their origins.[6] Our theological language, including our doctrinal language, is extremely important in bringing the church's faith to conceptual expression, but it remains a second order language, removed by one or more levels from the faith experience it seeks to express.

We can take a clue here from biblical theology, which is always careful to identify the literary form or type of literature of a passage. Those who like to browse in bookstores understand implicitly the principle of literary form. Even if they would be hard-pressed to define it properly, they would never confuse a historical novel with science fiction, or a theological text with a cookbook. They are simply different literary forms, different types of literature.

The Old Testament is rich in literary forms. They include poetry (epic, erotic, lyric, didactic, songs of praise, lamentations), myths, patriarchal legends, court histories, law codes, prophetic oracles, fictional tales, proverbs, and apocalyptic visions. Among New Testament literary forms we can find gospels, epistles, miracle stories, pronouncement stories, sayings of Jesus, liturgical formulas, parables, doxologies, stories about Jesus, historical narratives, apocalyptic sayings, and so forth. A particular passage in a gospel may reflect the actual words of

---

[6] See Congregation for the Doctrine of the Faith, "Declaration in Defense of the Catholic Doctrine on the Church against Certain Errors of the Present Day," *Origins* 3 (1973) 97–100.

Jesus, very early Christian preaching, the editorial or creative work of the evangelist, or a catechetical instruction or liturgical formula from an early Christian community. The evangelists could draw on any of this material, and several different literary forms may appear within a given passage.

Some stories, such as the adoration of the shepherds (Luke 2:15-20) or the twelve-year-old Jesus lecturing the teachers in the Temple (Luke 2:41-52), may be simply that—stories, not historical narratives—used to suggest the unique identity of this child. Miracle stories in the gospels reflect the community's memory that Jesus was known as a miracle worker, though some stories of healing reflect actual events. The more extraordinary, "nature" miracles like walking on water or changing water into wine are considered by many today to be ways of witnessing to Jesus' power over nature, thus intimations of his divinity. Such an approach is quite different from literalizing the story and then arguing: Jesus changed water into wine; therefore he is divine.

The image of the Son of Man coming on the clouds of heaven in judgment (Mark 14:62) is an apocalyptic image, perhaps used by Jesus to indicate his own role as judge; it does not necessarily point to a literal second coming. Many of the sayings of Jesus in the gospels reflect his very words (Latin: *ipsissima verba*), while others may have been fashioned by the evangelists on the basis of the Jesus tradition. Thus they are true to the spirit of his teaching but not literal repetitions of his words. Some of the Easter stories may have been fashioned by the evangelists to teach early communities that they too can encounter the risen Jesus in the breaking of the bread or Eucharist (Luke 24:13-35), or that they do not have to see with their own eyes, like Thomas, in order to believe (John 20:24-29). Behind them lies the even earlier Easter *kerygma* or proclamation, brief testimonies of the earliest Christians' absolute conviction that Jesus had been raised from the dead and there are witnesses (Acts 2:32-33; 5:30-31; 1 Cor 15:4-8). Thus, there is often a difference between the imagery or language used in a passage and the truth it intends to communicate.

In the Middle Ages Christian theology, influenced by the heritage of Greek reason, was often expressed in philosophical language. To illustrate the difference between what the faith community experiences and how it ultimately describes that experience in a language borrowed from philosophy and ultimately in doctrine, we will take as a practical example the church's belief in Christ's sacramental presence in the Eucharist.

Christ's Eucharistic Presence

The doctrine of Christ's "real" presence in the Eucharist offers an example of the differences between originating experience and its theological expression. Belief in Christ's unique eucharistic presence is at the heart of the Catholic tradition. And yet, though Catholic theology has used the language of substantial change, one does not find this kind of language in the New Testament. But it is clear from Catholic theology, popular Catholic faith, and Scripture itself that the Eucharist is much more than a mere remembrance of the Last Supper. Scripture speaks of a communion or participation (*koinōnia*) in the body and blood of Christ by sharing in the cup blessed and the bread broken (1 Cor 10:16), of recognizing the risen Jesus in the breaking of the bread (Luke 24:35), of discerning his body (1 Cor 11:29), in other words of meeting the risen Christ in the community's sacramental meal or Eucharist (1 Cor 1:16-17). In John's discourse on the Bread of Life, Jesus says, "Whoever eats my flesh and drinks my blood has eternal life, and I will raise him on the last day" (John 6:54). But even here the reference is to a meal.

From the second century on the fathers of the church used realistic language in referring to the body and blood of Christ. Ignatius of Antioch (d. 110) wrote that the Docetists, who denied that Christ was truly a human being, "abstain from eucharist (thanksgiving) and prayer, because they allow not that the eucharist is the flesh of our Savior Jesus Christ."[7] Justin (d. ca. 165) compared the union of the bread and wine with Christ's body and blood to the joining of the divine and human in the Incarnation:

> For not as common bread and common drink do we receive these; but in like manner as Jesus Christ our Savior, having been made flesh by the Word of God, had both flesh and blood for our salvation, so likewise have we been taught that the food which is blessed by the prayer of His word, and from which our blood and flesh by transmutation are nourished, is the flesh and blood of that Jesus who was made flesh.[8]

Ambrose (d. 397), arguing that the power of grace was superior to that of nature, spoke of a change of the elements: "We observe, then, that grace has more power than nature, and yet so far we have only spoken of the grace of a prophet's blessing. . . . But if the word of Elijah had

---

[7] Ignatius of Antioch, *Smyrneans* 6.7.

[8] Irenaeus, *First Apology*, 66.

such power as to bring down fire from heaven, shall not the word of Christ have power to change the nature of the elements?" (*On the Mysteries*, 52).

The language of substantial change (transubstantiation) emerged in the eleventh century because of a theological dispute. Berengar (d. 1088), a theologian who was head of the school of St. Martin at Tours in France, seems to have taught that Christ was present in the Eucharist *only* as sign, rather than that the bread was identical with his body. His approach was seen as overly symbolic, denying Christ's real presence. The confession imposed on him by the Council of Rome (1059) seems to us today as overly literal; as David Power says, "who today would care to state that communicants chew on the body of Christ?"[9] The term "transubstantiation" was used by the Fourth Lateran Council (1215) to affirm that while the appearances of the bread and wine remained the same, the substance of both really changed.

The Council of Trent adopted transubstantiation as an "appropriate" (*aptissime*) way of talking about what happens in the Eucharist (DS 1642), but it is not the only way. The council's real concern, evident in its canons, was the reality of Christ's presence. It did not commit the church to a scholastic analysis of change or to scholastic categories. Canon 1 affirms that in the Eucharist the whole Christ, body and blood, soul and divinity are contained truly, really, and substantially (DS 1651). In other words, what is present is the risen Jesus himself, not his discrete flesh and blood. If Christ is present sacramentally rather than physically, his presence is more than sign or figure; he is truly encountered as a person, not chewed or digested as a thing.

If Trent safeguarded belief in Christ's real, sacramental presence, its emphasis on substantial change led to an unfortunate shift from attention on Christ's presence in the gifts and the eucharistic assembly to a one-sided emphasis on the transformation of the elements. While some Christian traditions have lost sight of Christ's sacramental presence and rarely celebrate the Eucharist, Catholics have often used an overly literal language to express their eucharistic faith, including expressions such as "the miracle of transubstantiation" or pious stories of bleeding hosts.

Power argues that the idea of substantial change was used because it seemed integral to the idea of substantial presence. But again, it is only

---

[9] David N. Power, *The Eucharistic Mystery: Revitalizing the Tradition* (New York: Crossroad, 1992) 244; DS 690.

one way of explaining the sacramental action, expressed differently by the Reformers and still discussed by theologians today. Many Catholics are unaware that some Protestant traditions clearly recognize that Christ is present in the sacramental bread and the wine, though they may express it differently. "Trent's teaching on substantial change, Luther's analogy with the doctrine of the Incarnation, his appeal to Christ's Lordship that led him to compare Christ's sacramental presence with God's ubiquity, and Calvin's teaching on a presence of Christ through the power of the Spirit are three different ways of trying to explain the one mystery in which fundamentally all professed faith and belief."[10]

Doctrine and Theological Traditions

What is the relation between theology and doctrine? Doctrine (Latin, *doctrina*, teaching) is the word used for official church teaching. It is an expression of belief that the church has made its own by some authoritative act of its teaching office or magisterium. "Doctrines express judgments of fact and judgments of value."[11] They are different from theologians' opinions and are owed an *obsequium religiosum* (LG 25), a term variously translated as religious assent, submission, or obedience. Religious assent indicates primarily a predisposition to receive graciously, to submit to what is taught by authority.

A dogma is a doctrine that has been solemnly defined by the church's highest authority as divinely revealed. For Roman Catholics dogmas include the articles of the Creed, the solemn teachings of the ecumenical councils, and the *ex cathedra* (infallible) teachings of the extraordinary papal magisterium or the teachings of the ordinary and universal magisterium, the last a category more difficult to identify.[12] Dogmas demand a submission of faith; to reject a dogma would be to place oneself outside the community of faith, for a community without common beliefs is no longer cohesive.

Doctrines can develop, be reinterpreted, and occasionally change or be "reformed." For example, the teaching about "no salvation outside the Church" (*extra ecclesia nulla salus*) was changed by the Second Vatican

---

[10] Power, *The Eucharistic Mystery*, 255–256 at 256.

[11] Bernard J. F. Lonergan, *Method in Theology* (New York: Herder and Herder, 1972) 132.

[12] See Francis A. Sullivan, *Creative Fidelity: Weighing and Interpreting Documents of the Magisterium* (New York: Paulist Press, 1996) 102–110.

Council, which acknowledged that God's grace is effective beyond the parameters of the Christian community (LG 16). Dogmas can be reinterpreted, but not changed; they are "irreformable." The Second Vatican Council reinterpreted Vatican I's teaching on papal infallibility by placing it in the broader context of its theology of episcopal collegiality (LG 25), but it did not deny what Vatican I had taught.

Theological Traditions

After almost two thousand years Christianity is rich in theological traditions. In addition to its Scriptures and its popular traditions, its faith is expressed in doctrines, creeds, confessions, and liturgies, in the works of theologians and theological schools, and in more recent times in agreed statements resulting from ecumenical dialogues between churches. The Catholic tradition in particular appears to some as doctrinally "heavy." Catholics remain bound by doctrinal expressions of faith that have attained dogmatic status; for most Protestants such teachings remain simply theology. Thus Protestant traditions, built on the Reformation principle of "Scripture alone," sometimes seem more free.

But Protestant faith also is shaped by theological statements and confessions. This is particularly true of the confessional churches. Lutheran Christianity remains strongly committed to Martin Luther's insight that we are justified by faith alone, not by works of the law. To this day, the doctrine of justification by faith remains the basic Lutheran confession as well as the *articulus stantis et cadentis ecclesiae*, the article by which the church stands or falls.[13] For many Lutherans, this one principle serves to relativize other theological doctrines or practices.

Reformed Christianity in its various forms—Reformed, Presbyterian, United Church as well as in many Baptist and evangelical expressions—is still strongly informed by the theology of John Calvin, expressed in his *Institutes of the Christian Religion*.[14] An extreme form of his theology, often called "hyper-Calvinism," has been summarized in five doctrines: total depravity, unconditional election, limited atonement, irresistible grace,

---

[13] See *Justification by Faith: Lutherans and Catholics in Dialogue VII*: edited by H. George Anderson, T. Austin Murphy, and Joseph A. Burgess (Minneapolis, MN: Augsburg Publishing House, 1985) no. 117; for a more nuanced view, see Lutheran-Catholic Dialogue, "Joint Declaration on the Doctrine of Justification," *Origins* 28, no. 8 (1998) Appendix, For 3.

[14] John Calvin, *Institutes of the Christian Religion*, 2 vols., ed. John T. McNeill (Philadelphia: The Westminster Press, 1960).

and perseverance of the saints.[15] Conservative evangelicals often insist on a narrow interpretation of justification that is explained in terms of sinful rebellion, substitutionary satisfaction, imputed righteousness, forensic declaration, and eternal punishment without personal faith in Christ.[16]

Pentecostals, with their greater insistence on life in the Spirit, are an exception here; Pentecostal Christianity is more experiential; the experience of life in the Spirit is more important than its rational articulation. Many conservative evangelicals, lacking an effective magisterium that can rethink traditional positions in the light of new evidence and theological development, remain committed to a doctrine of biblical inerrancy which in the final analysis is more confessional than biblical; they attribute an infallibility to the biblical text that Catholics would not dream of attributing to the pope.

Doctrinal differences and boundaries can cause divisions within a tradition when they are misunderstood, interpreted in an overly literal way, or taken out of their proper context. They can also make conversations across traditions difficult.

Conclusion

If there is a critical as well as a constructive dimension to theology, it remains a work of the church, refining the church's religious language in light of its tradition, always in communion with the community of faith. Doctrines are those theological formulas which the church has made its own. Dogmas are doctrines which articulate the parameters of the community's belief, its "rule of faith," expressed in creeds and solemn definitions.

All our theological statements, even dogmatic ones, are limited expressions of truth. They are conditioned by the cultures, concerns, and conceptualities of their time of origin. Our theological languages represent efforts to express in concept and symbol what the early Christians experienced in faith. It is not easy to separate theology from faith, because to put our knowledge and experience of God into language is to interpret it, to theologize. Still, theology remains a second order language, removed by one or more levels of abstraction from the experience out

---

[15] See Edwin H. Palmer, *The Five Points of Calvinism* (Grand Rapids, MI: Baker House, 1972).

[16] "The Gospel of Jesus Christ: An Evangelical Celebration," *Christianity Today* 43, no. 7 (January 10, 1999) 51–56.

of which it developed. We saw an example of this in the church's theological language about Christ's eucharistic presence.

Recently, some weeks into a new course, I gave my students an article by Daniel Migliore entitled "The Task of Theology."[17] Their assignment was to discuss how one "does" theology, and then to illustrate it in terms of what we had done so far in the course. The article emphasized the critical, questioning nature of theology; that it does not mean the repetition of traditional doctrines but a genuine search for the truth, that faith and inquiry are inseparable, that the theologian who remains satisfied with unexamined beliefs too easily slips into ideology, superstition, fanaticism, or idolatry.

But Migliore is too good a theologian to reduce theology to an endless search for truth. He defines theology "as a continuing search for the fullness of the truth of God made known in Jesus Christ."[18] He stresses that genuine knowledge of God is inseparable from worship and service (Calvin), that too much theology, or a theology that gets lost in idle speculations or academic trivialities is fruitless, like the divine judgment delivered by Amos on Israelite feasts, sacrifices, and songs offered up without conversion of the heart and justice for the poor (Karl Barth, cf. Amos 5:21-24), that theology must continue to ask what powers it is serving and whose interests it is promoting.

When I read the students' papers I found that almost all of them resonated with Migliore's emphasis on questioning. But only two mentioned that theology was concerned with truth, that it dealt with what God had revealed. My students were very much children of their age, individualistic, subjective, having little sense that there is any truth communicated by faith. It was "what I think," or "my interpretation," or "what is true for me." One said, "theology is the study of faith, and faith is up to the interpretation of the individual." Another, acknowledging that she rarely went to church, said, "I've always believed in God as an individual communicator, and I didn't learn about him through school or church, but experiences and people."

For the Christian, the Creed is not just theology. It is the church's confession of faith, rooted in Scripture and the baptismal formularies of the primitive church. The Creed constitutes the church's rule of faith. It can never be a mere statement of opinion. Unlike the contemporary

---

[17] Daniel L. Migliore, *Faith Seeking Understanding: An Introduction to Christian Theology* (Grand Rapids, MI: William B. Eerdmans, 2004) 1–9.

[18] Ibid., 1.

Christian who may rattle off the Creed reflexively with the Sunday congregation, the Apostles' Creed once formed the basis of a solemn commitment made liturgically after several years of catechesis, prayer, and reflection, the remnants of which we have today in the Rite of Christian Initiation for Adults (RCIA).

Even more, to recite the Creed is to enter into a relationship. To say "I believe in God, the Father almighty" is to address the God whose very Otherness can bring us to our knees in reverence and awe, the transcendent God we come to know as Father, Son, and Holy Spirit. It is time to turn to the Creed.

God

Chapter 3

"I believe in God"

The Apostles' Creed begins with the confession, "I believe (Latin: *credo*) in God." But how can we know or believe in a God we cannot see or directly experience? Our knowledge begins always in experience. The Gospel of John tells us, "No one has ever seen God. The only Son, God, who is at the Father's side, has revealed him" (John 1:18).

Given the apparent distance between ourselves and God, how can we understand something of the divine mystery without some divine word? The German Jesuit Karl Rahner, one of the most influential theologians of the twentieth century, defines the human person as a "hearer of the word," that is, one who listens for God's revealing word.[1] Jews, Christians, and Muslims, the "Peoples of the Book," believe that God has spoken a word to humankind; they see the beginning of God's self-communication in the experience of Israel, a tribe of nomads wandering with their flocks in the deserts of the ancient Middle East. We call their sacred literature the Old Testament. We begin our profession of faith with the revelation of God in the Old Testament. However, the word we receive cannot be anything but a partial disclosure. Before considering the God of Israel, we need to consider more closely the nature of the divine mystery.

The Incomprehensibility of God

Towards the end of his life Rahner began to speak increasingly about the "incomprehensibility" of God. By this he meant that God remains so

---

[1] Karl Rahner, *Hearers of the Word* (New York: Herder and Herder, 1969).

different, so "other," so transcendent that to the finite, created human intellect God remains mystery. Basing his argument on the teaching of Thomas Aquinas, Rahner maintained that the disparity between the infinite being of God and the finite intellect is so great that even in the immediate vision of God, the beatific vision to which we look forward in faith, God cannot be comprehended or understood.[2]

In fact, God's incomprehensibility actually increases because the beatific vision reveals God's total simplicity. What we come to know is not some finite, created idea (species) or determinate essence, but God as pure subsistent being (*ipsum esse subsistens*). God is absolute, necessary being, pure existence whose "essence" is to be, while all other beings are contingent, finite beings in which existence (the "to be") and essence (the "whatness" of their being) are distinct. Thus the attribution of incomprehensibility to God is really a statement about the finite, limited character of human knowing, a characteristic teaching of medieval theologians. For example, Anselm of Canterbury compares the light in which God dwells to the sun, blinding the human intellect:

> Surely, Lord, inaccessible light is your dwelling place, for no one apart from yourself can enter into it and fully comprehend you. If I fail to see this light it is simply because it is too bright for me. Still, it is by this light that I do see all that I can, even as weak eyes, unable to look straight at the sun, see all that they can by the sun's light.[3]

Rahner's theological anthropology leads him to speak of human beings also as incomprehensible. The very structure of our cognition reveals that in every act of knowing we necessarily experience a transcendence that reaches beyond the objects known to a horizon which remains infinite. Thus our knowing implicitly raises questions about all reality, the infinite, being as such which remains in some way grasped ("unthematically," "pre-apprehended") but still beyond our direct experience. Our knowledge is always limited, our love imperfect, our joys transitory, our life itself in all its vitality limited by the knowledge of inevitable death. And yet our consciousness extends beyond any being, love, or joy to wonder about the perfect, the full, and the eternal. In this "unfilled transcendentality," Rahner reasons, the human person is

---

[2] See for example, Karl Rahner, "Thomas Aquinas on the Incomprehensibility of God," *Journal of Religion* 58 Supplement (1978) S107–125.

[3] Anselm, *Proslogion*, 16.

revealed as an unanswered question to itself, constantly transcending the horizons of its own knowing, and thus as spirit.[4]

Of course few are willing to grant the spiritual character of the human person today. And the very concept of divine incomprehensibility may sound strange in an age in which many speak as though they had intimate knowledge of the divine purpose and nature. Thus fundamentalist preachers call down God's coming judgment on sinners in the form of earthquakes or tidal waves, usually for sexual sins, and apocalyptic writers of theological fiction like Tim LaHaye and Jerry Jenkins describe in great detail the coming "rapture" in their *Left Behind* series. At the same time, countless people who proclaim, "I'm spiritual but not religious," fashion for themselves a god of their own choosing, without benefit of any mediating tradition, whether biblical or ecclesiastical. They risk creating comfortable gods in their own image, gods who make no demands. Thus does our age seek to domesticate the divine.

The biblical tradition is very different. From the beginning, in spite of the fact that the Bible often uses anthropomorphic language, it insists that God is not "like us." God is "wholly other," beyond the ability of our minds to grasp or comprehend. Theology speaks of this as God's transcendence. The Decalogue forbids attempting to represent God by means of images (Exod 20:4; cf. Deut 5:8). Moses, in awe before the burning bush, is told: "Come no nearer! Remove the sandals from your feet, for the place where you stand is holy ground" (Exod 3:5). Afraid to look at God, Moses hides his face, for he has encountered what Rudolf Otto calls the holy, the mystery both terrifying and fascinating.[5] Mere mortals cannot look on the face of God and live (Exod 19:21; 33:20). In the presence of the holy they fall down in fear and trembling, like the disciples on the mount of the transfiguration (Mark 9:6) or like Peter in the story of the miraculous catch of fish; they are overwhelmed with the knowledge of their own sinfulness (Luke 5:1-11).

The book of Job is a marvelous meditation on God who remains mystery. Job is the just man, not perfect, but "a blameless and upright man . . . who feared God and avoided evil" (Job 1:1). Challenged by Satan, who appears here as a member of the heavenly court with the office of testing human virtue, God allows him to have complete power over Job, sparing only his life. When a series of tragedies strikes Job,

---

[4] See Karl Rahner, *Foundations of Christian Faith: An Introduction to the Idea of Christianity* (New York: Seabury Press, 1978) 31–35.

[5] Rudolf Otto, *The Idea of the Holy* (New York: Oxford University Press, 1958).

taking from him wealth, family, and health, his friends gather around him, urging him to acknowledge his guilt. Job remains steadfast in maintaining his innocence. He refuses to criticize God, saying only, "The LORD gave and the LORD has taken away; / blessed be the name of the LORD!" (Job 1:21). Finally however, goaded by the relentless criticism of his friends, Job demands of God an explanation. Really a *crie du coeur* that challenges the popular view that God punishes the wicked and rewards the just with prosperity, Job's demand for an answer surfaces powerfully the mystery of the suffering and evil that befalls the just man or woman. The later books of the Old Testament wrestled with this mystery, particularly in the Wisdom literature, but were never able to give an adequate answer.

Finally, in some of the most beautiful poetry in the Old Testament, God answers Job from out of the whirlwind:

> Who is this that obscures divine plans
>   with words of ignorance?
> Gird up your loins now, like a man;
>   I will question you, and you tell me the answers!
> Where were you when I founded the earth?
>   Tell me, if you have understanding.
> Who determined its size; do you know?
>   Who stretched out the measuring line for it?
> Into what were its pedestals sunk,
>   and who laid the cornerstone,
> While the morning stars sang in chorus
>   and all the sons of God shouted for joy?
>
> And who shut within doors the sea,
>   when it burst forth from the womb;
> When I made the clouds its garment
>   and thick darkness its swaddling bands?
> When I set limits for it
>   and fastened the bar of its door,
> And said: Thus far shall you come but no farther,
>   and here shall your proud waves be stilled!
>
> Have you ever in your lifetime commanded the morning
>   and shown the dawn its place
> For taking hold of the ends of the earth,
>   till the wicked are shaken from its surface? . . .

Have you fitted a curb to the Pleiades,
    or loosened the bonds of Orion?
Can you bring forth the Mazzaroth in their season,
    or guide the Bear with its train?
Do you know the ordinances of the heavens;
    can you put into effect their plan on the earth?
                          (Job 38:2-13; 31-33)

God's answer to Job is to point to the mysteries of creation and, by implication, the divine incomprehensibility. So Job acknowledges that he has dealt with things he does not understand, with things he cannot know (Job 42:3).

The God of Israel

Before we begin to consider the God of Israel, we need to make a methodological prelude. Considered as a whole, the Old Testament is an extremely complex work of literature, some forty-six books in the Catholic canon, thirty-nine in the Protestant.[6] Composed over a period of almost a thousand years, the diverse Hebrew books include equally diverse theologies. Because of this, any unity imposed, whether in terms of concepts such as covenant, Law, messianism, wisdom, or sacred history, risks rationalizing from a Christian perspective what remains the rich religious experience of the people we call, somewhat inaccurately, Israel. If anything gives unity to Israel's experience, it is Israel's God, Yahweh.[7]

Without imposing a rigid "sacred history" interpretation upon Israel's experience of Yahweh, we will seek to recover the Israelite experience of their God against a general historical framework, if for no other reason than that Israel's experience of Yahweh in history "often consisted of hearing the prophetic interpretation of history," and the Israelites believed that their history was the work of their God.[8] From their diverse testimonies to their historical experience of God we can gain insight into

---

[6] The Reformers dropped from the Protestant canon the seven "Deuterocanonical" Jewish books which they call "the Apocrypha"; not found in the Jewish canon because they were in Greek rather than Hebrew, they had been part of the canon of the Church since the beginning.

[7] See John L. McKenzie, *A Theology of the Old Testament* (Garden City, NY: Image Books, 1976) 22–32.

[8] McKenzie, *A Theology of the Old Testament*, 35.

the God of Israel who was the God of Jesus. In other words, who is this God about whom we profess, "I believe"?

Naming the Divine

The story of Israel begins with the patriarch Abraham who migrated with his clan from Mesopotamia to Canaan or Palestine towards the end of the second millennium (Gen 12:1-4). Abraham worshiped a tribal or clan deity, as did his descendants.

The Bible identifies the God of the patriarchs variously as the God of Abraham, the God of Isaac, or the God of Jacob.[9] The names were often personalized as "the Awesome One of Isaac" (Gen 31:42) or "the Mighty One of Jacob" (Gen 49:24). As the God of a nomadic people rather than a local deity, this patriarchal God traveled with the clan. Israel's relation with God was personal rather than formal and institutional; God's presence was not confined to a shrine or place. This dynamic relationship would later find expression in the notion of covenant.

As the ancestors of the Hebrews settled in the land of Canaan they encountered a universal God, El (sometimes the plural form Elohim was used), worshiped by the inhabitants at various shrines. Originally the generic word for deity in Semitic languages, it became personalized at various sanctuaries or shrines in Canaan: at Jerusalem as El Elyon (God the Most High), at Beer-sheba as El Olam (God Eternal), and at Shechem as El Berith (God of the Covenant). The ancestors of Israel (Isra-el = God has saved) also began worshiping their God under the name of El at these shrines. An early name was El Shaddai (Gen 17:1), translated in the Septuagint as "Almighty" (Greek *pantokratōr*), though some scholars believe the name once meant "The One of the Mountain." Thus, long before the ancestors of Israel knew God as Yahweh they worshiped a God who combined the personal character of the God of the patriarchs with the universal characteristics of El, the supreme God of the Canaanites.

The name Yahweh, said to have been introduced by Moses (Exod 3:13-14), appears in the Exodus story in the context of its theology of the covenant. It is the personal name for the God of Israel whose worship came to Canaan with the conquest. The exact meaning of the name in Hebrew is uncertain. Derived from the root *hayah*, "to be," it is given

---

[9] In this section I am following John L. McKenzie, "Aspects of Old Testament Thought," the *New Jerome Biblical Commentary*, ed. Raymond E. Brown, Joseph A. Fitzmyer, and Roland E. Murphy (Englewood Cliffs, NJ: Prentice Hall, 1990) 1285–87.

in the first person as "I am who I am" in Exodus 3:14. The Septuagint Greek gave it a more philosophical translation as "I am he that is," while Jerome translated it as "I am who am" in the Vulgate. This enigmatic name YHWH designates not the god of a land or place but, as Pope Benedict XVI comments, simply God, without qualification: "This God simply *is*. When he says 'I am,' he is presenting himself precisely as the one who is, in his utter oneness."[10]

So holy was this name that in the late pre-Christian period the Jews would not pronounce it. Later in their texts they combined the "Tetragrammaton," the four consonants of *YHWH* (Hebrew was written without the vowels) with the superscripted vowels from Adonai, reminding the synagogue reader to substitute Adonai, "Lord," for the sacred name. This led to a misreading of the name as "Jehovah" in the sixteenth century. The correct vocalization for YHWH is most likely "Jahweh" or "Yahweh."[11]

Were the ancient Israelites strict monotheists? In the ancient Near East a multiplicity of divine beings was taken for granted. Still Israel's experience was unique. Not a speculative people, they were practical, not theoretical monotheists. They worshiped Yahweh and Yahweh alone (Exod 20:3; Deut 5:7-9). Next to Yahweh, the Elohim or gods of other peoples were insignificant, without real power. The first clear denial of the existence of other gods comes in Second Isaiah in the sixth century BCE, though some scholars see evidence of this even earlier, as in Deuteronomy 32:39.

While the Israelites often used strongly anthropomorphic language to describe their God, it was clear that Yahweh was completely different from human beings. The word "holy," from the Hebrew root *qds*, refers to God's otherness, difference, or apartness from created reality, which by definition is limited and imperfect. So great was God's otherness that to look upon God's face was to die (Exod 33:20; cf. 2 Sam 6:6-8). In a charming story, Moses asks Yahweh, "Do let me see your glory!" The Lord responds that "no man sees me and still lives." But he places Moses in the hollow of the rock, covers him with his hand, and passes by "so that you may see my back; but my face is not to be seen" (Exod 33:18-23). The story says something about Moses' intimate relationship with God. It also suggests that we get only glimpses of the divine mystery, partial insights into God's incomprehensibility; we often recognize God only

---

[10] Joseph Ratzinger/Pope Benedict XVI, *Jesus of Nazareth: From the Baptism in the Jordan to the Transfiguration* (New York: Doubleday, 2007) 348.

[11] Many modern English translations use the upper case LORD to indicate that the name Yahweh appears in the Hebrew.

in retrospect, when God has been present, but we cannot look on God directly. And yet the Israelites rejoiced in God's presence, as is so clear from the psalms. Reading the psalms is to open a window to the public prayer and religious experience of Israel.

Related to God's holiness or otherness was the prohibition of images of God "in the shape of anything in the sky above or on the earth below or in the waters beneath the earth" (Exod 20:4; cf. Deut 5:8; cf. Lev 26:1). This too was unique in the ancient Near East. Unlike the gods of the nations, the God of normative Yahwism did not have a sexual partner or enter into sexual relations with humans like the gods of the Greeks. What is interesting is that the ancient Israelites, lacking the language and conceptuality which would describe God as spirit, nevertheless articulated a vision of a God who was unlike anything else in the universe. God was at once transcendent and immanent, present in their history and other. God could not be seen or represented by any artifact. No image of Yahweh has ever been found.

There was also a strong moral dimension to the Israelite experience of God, for God's people also were to be holy. "Be holy, for I, the LORD, your God, am holy" (Lev 19:2). Thus the Israelites struggled against any religious syncretism; they did not practice child sacrifice as some ancient peoples in Canaan seem to have done (Lev 20:2-5); nor were they allowed to take part in the fertility cults of their Canaanite neighbors, a cult which symbolized the annual renewal of fertility by sexual intercourse between the god and his consort, represented by the temple priests and priestesses as well as by the worshipers, who joined in the ritual fornication.

God and God's People

From what we have seen Israel did not first think of God as a creator or first cause of the visible world. Their God was a clan or tribal deity who accompanied the people in their wandering and trials, the God of the patriarchs. "I am with you" is a constant refrain (Gen 26:24; 28:15; Josh 3:7; Isa 41:10; Jer 15:20), assuring the people and their leaders of God's presence on their behalf. While they were familiar with creation stories from their neighbors and saw creation as part of God's salvific work, specific texts about God as creator are generally considered to date from the exile or later.

The two great traditions of the book of Exodus, the Exodus itself and the covenant of Sinai, welded Israel into a people, God's people. As immigrants, they had experienced oppression and exploitation in Egypt. Under the leadership of Moses they departed that land of tears as "a crowd of mixed ancestry" (Exod 12:38)—fugitive slaves, people of other tribes, even some Egyptians. Thus the salvation celebrated in the Passover Supper was a symbol of God's salvation from political and social oppression. Through the Sinai tradition, with Moses functioning as a prophet, they learned that God was their deliverer or savior who had entered into a relationship or covenant with them: "I the LORD, am your God, who brought you out of the land of Egypt, that place of slavery. You shall not have other gods besides me" (Exod 20:2-3). This sense of being chosen as God's own people was to remain the fundamental religious experience for those in the Jewish tradition (cf. Deut 26:5-9).

As they settled into the land of Canaan various social, political, and economic interests brought together the diverse peoples who became Israel—those that had shared the Exodus experience, others who joined them in the land, and no doubt some Canaanites who had originally resisted this influx of newcomers. But the real bond that united them was religious, the worship of Yahweh and the terms of the covenant, spelled out in the Decalogue (Exod 20:2-17; Deut 5:6-21). Solemn ceremonies such as the one at Shechem described in Joshua 24 ritually incorporated whole communities into covenant relationship with Yahweh and Israel. As the tribes had no central government, no monarch, they saw Yahweh as their true king. This notion of the kingship of Yahweh was gradually extended over the other nations, and finally over creation itself. Thus the earthly power of kingship became a symbol for the power and rule of God even after Israel developed its own monarchy.

Shift to the Future

Israel became a monarchy around 1030 BCE to meet the crisis of the invading Philistines. Its ideal king would remain David, who for a while was able to unite the ten northern tribes with the southern tribes of Judah and Benjamin, making the Jebusite city Jerusalem its capital. But a united Israel was not able to survive his successor Solomon, and in 922 the kingdom lapsed into the old divisions, with Israel in the North and Judah in the South.

The subsequent history of the two kingdoms is not a happy one. With weak kings, greedy upper classes, and the constant threat of religious syncretism, the people did not remain faithful to God's covenant. A long series of prophets tried to call them to conversion, both personal and national, rebuking them for their worship of other gods, for the injustice that made life so difficult for the poor, and for trusting in foreign alliances rather than

Yahweh. A common image for their apostasy was adultery; Israel had not been faithful to Yahweh her spouse (Hos 4:1-2; Ezek 16; 23).

There is much to be learned from the prophetic preaching. While they were not against the cult (Third Isaiah may be an exception here), they criticized a religion of ritual and cult when it did not lead to conversion of heart and justice for the poor. God's concern for the poor—for the widow, the orphan, the stranger in the land—present in much of the Old Testament (Exod 22:24-26; Lev 25:35-55), emerges with a special clarity in the prophets and will reappear in Jesus' preaching about the kingdom of God. In the southern kingdom of Judah, Nathan's promise that a future son of David would inherit an everlasting kingdom (2 Sam 7:11-16) led to a false confidence in the national life (Jer 7:1-11).

Ultimately, the prophets were unsuccessful; the judgment they warned about came true when the northern kingdom of Israel fell to the Assyrians in 722, to be followed by the destruction of Judah, Jerusalem, and the Temple at the hands of the Babylonians in 587 with the subsequent exile of the people. But their preaching, never without an element of hope that God would not abandon the people, affected a dramatic shift in their religious imagination, away from what God had done in the past and towards an expectation of a new, definitive intervention in their life. Variously expressed, they spoke of a new Davidic king or "messiah" (anointed) who would govern wisely and bring justice for the poor and the oppressed (Isa 11:1-9; Jer 23:5; Zech 9:9). Or of a Day of Yahweh when God's judgment would be revealed (Isa 2:11; Joel 4:14). Ezekiel spoke of a renewal of the covenant (Ezek 34:25; 37:26), while Jeremiah predicted that God would make a new covenant with the people (Jer 31:31-34).

The "Servant Songs" of Second Isaiah celebrate the mysterious figure of the Suffering Servant of Yahweh who would bring forth justice for the nations (Isa 42:1-9; 49:1-7; 50:4-9) and give his life as an offering for sin (Isa 52:13–53:12). The result of the prophetic preaching is that Israel began to look to the future for God's salvation, rather than to the past, a shift that becomes explicit in Isaiah: "Remember not the events of the past, / the things of long ago consider not; / See, I am doing something new!" (Isa 43:18-19).[12]

---

[12] Some prophetic passages dear to Christians because of their Christological reference, among them Isa 7:14; 42:1-4; 53:13; 61:1; Jer 31:31; Micah 5:2; Hosea 11:1; Zech 9:9; 11:13, are generally excluded from the haftarot, the Jewish lectionary read on the Sabbath and feast days; see Hananel Mack, "What Happened to Jesus' Haftarah?" *Haaretz* (September 22, 2005) Elul 18, 5765.

Late Old Testament Judaism

This theological shift to salvation as God's future introduces the concept of the end times, or eschatology (from the Greek *eschatos*, for last or end), thus a spiritualization of the understanding of salvation. In the last two centuries before the time of Jesus, external pressure resulted in Jewish eschatological thinking taking on the more radical form of apocalyptic. During the persecution under Antiochus IV (167–164 BCE), Jews were being put to death when they did not renounce their faith. In this context they began to look forward to a dramatic intervention when God would bring the present order to a close, ushering in a new age and raising the dead to life. Predicting a final cataclysm, Daniel says:

> Many of those who sleep
> > in the dust of the earth shall awake;
> Some shall live forever,
> > others shall be an everlasting horror and disgrace.
> But the wise shall shine brightly
> > like the splendor of the firmament,
> And those who lead the many to justice
> > shall be like the stars forever.
> > > (Dan 12:2-3; cf. 2 Macc 12:44)

Also late in the Old Testament period one begins to find in the Wisdom literature more hints that God destined humankind for a life beyond the grave. Even earlier, the book of Job had wrestled with the suffering of the just one, without really offering any answer, beyond the incomprehensible mystery of the creator, as we have seen. But the book of Wisdom, most probably written in the last half of the first century BCE, looks beyond the traditional view that a relationship with Yahweh ends with death. The second chapter presents a meditation on the "just one," who becomes obnoxious to the wicked because he reproaches them for their transgressions and violations of the law (Wis 2:12). Because he styles himself "a child of the LORD" (Wis 2:13) who claims "that God is his Father" (Wis 2:16), they "condemn him to a shameful death; / for according to his own words, God will take care of him" (Wis 2:20). The chapter ends by saying that "God formed man to be imperishable; / the image of his own nature he made him. / But by the envy of the devil, death entered the world (Wis 2:23-24).

The prophetic and Wisdom traditions personified the divine agency in a way that shaped the Christian understanding of God. The prophetic tradition saw the word of God as a personification of the divine power, going forth from God to accomplish the divine purpose (Isa 55:11). The Wisdom tradition personified the divine Wisdom as a feminine figure active in the world, coming forth from the mouth of God (Sir 24:3), playing a role in creation (Sir 1:4; Prov 8:22-23), reflecting God's glory, an image of God's goodness (Wis 7:25-26). Sent forth from heaven, Wisdom makes her dwelling in Israel, where God is said to choose the spot for her tent (Sir 24:8-12).

Conclusion

What is amazing to us even today is the notion of God which emerges from the total experience of Israel, from its early days as a wandering group of nomads, through the later crises in their national life, down to the expectation of a new manifestation of God's grace that characterized much of first-century Palestinian Judaism. It was precisely *through* their historical experience that their understanding of God developed, or in more theological terms, that God's revelation or self-disclosure was mediated. If they borrowed freely from the theologies of their neighbors, they also purified them; they saw God as active in their nomadic and later national life, learned from the prophetic figures who reinterpreted their tradition in light of historical events and crises, finally broadening their notion of covenantal life with Yahweh so that the very late tradition includes the hope that God would raise the dead to life.

The concept of God that emerges is very different from that of their neighbors. Israel's God was transcendent, holy, beyond imagining or images. The very name, Yahweh, suggested God's otherness, God's incomprehensibility. Yet this God was also immanent, present in the life of the people, and demanded that they also be holy.

There are various passages in the Old Testament that might suggest a less gracious God, particularly for those with a more literal approach. For example, we read in Exodus that God was ready to kill Moses because he remained uncircumcised (Exod 4:24). Or that Moses had to convince God not to destroy the people in the wilderness at Sinai after they worshiped the golden calf (Exod 32:10). The ancient Israelite practice of the ban (Hb *herem*), putting to the sword men, livestock, even women and children in cities captured in wartime (1 Sam 15:1-10) or even Israelites who worshiped false gods (Deut 13:7-12)—all this was attributed to the divine command. So was the Deluge or great flood, sent by God according to Genesis because of human lawlessness (Gen 6:11-13). Yes, there are passages that reflect earlier stages in the tradition and later justifications for the violence unleashed by tribal conflicts and war. But a theology built on such isolated passages would present a false image of Israel's God; it loses the forest for the trees.

The God who emerges from the total experience of Israel, reflected in its Scriptures, is a God of compassion and love. It is a God who commands the harvesters not to "second pick" the field, so that the poor might feed themselves with what is left over (Deut 24:19-21), who commands Sabbatical years for the forgiveness of debts (Deut 15:1-3), the resting of the land and the relief of the poor (Exod 23:10-11), a God who commands the man who takes his neighbor's cloak as a pledge on a loan to return it at sunset, so that he has covering for his body in the cold of the desert night, and who says, "If he cries out to me, I will hear him; for I am compassionate" (Exod 22:26). This God calls Israel to a similar compassion:

> This, rather, is the fasting that I wish:
> releasing those bound unjustly,
> untying the thongs of the yoke;
> Setting free the oppressed,
> breaking every yoke;
> Sharing your bread with the hungry,
> sheltering the oppressed and the homeless;
> Clothing the naked when you see them,
> and not turning your back on your own.
> (Isa 58:6-7)

The command not to wrong the widow, the orphan, or the stranger in the land echoes constantly through both the Law (the Pentateuch) and the prophets. This is the God who says, "it is love that I desire, not sacrifice" (Hos 6:6; cf. Matt 12:7). It is this God who is the God of Jesus, as we will see in the next chapter.

Chapter 4

"The Father almighty"

A common misapprehension is that the God of the Old Testament is a stern God of law and wrath, while the God of Jesus is a God of love and compassion. One finds this claim as early as the year 150 CE, when the priest Marcion, influenced by Gnosticism, used it in his effort to reject the Jewish Scriptures from their use in Christian worship. But nothing could be further from the truth, as we saw in the last chapter. The God of the Old Testament is the God of Jesus, the God he called Father. In the Creed we call God Father as well.

The God of Jesus

Jesus came to know this God as a young Jew growing up in Nazareth. He would have learned about God from his parents and from the elders of the village who schooled him in the Jewish tradition. This was the God he sought in his prayer, the God of Israel, the God of the Law and the prophets.

When he heard about John the Baptist, he traveled from Galilee to the Jordan near Jericho where John was preaching and baptizing. Baptized himself, something happened to him through that experience. He didn't return immediately to his former life, but stayed awhile in John's company. After some time Jesus began his own ministry, with his own disciples. But his message was different from John's. John had stressed a coming judgment. Though Jesus also called his listeners to a conversion of life, his preaching was more joyful; it was genuinely "the gospel

[Greek: *euangelion*, "good news"] of God" (Mark 1:14). He proclaimed that the reign of God was at hand, evident in his ministry, bringing comfort and hope to many. He healed those suffering from sickness or troubled by evil spirits. He restored to the community those who had been marginalized because of physical illness or violation of the laws of religious purity. He proclaimed forgiveness to sinners. His message was good news for the poor (Luke 4:18-19). His open table fellowship symbolized that no one was excluded from God's reign and led to the frequent criticism, this man eats with tax collectors and sinners (Mark 2:16; Matt 11:19).

God's special concern for the poor is one of the most characteristic themes in Jesus' preaching. In the Beatitudes he proclaims the poor, the hungry, and the sorrowing blessed of God (Luke 6:20-26; cf. Matt 5:1-12). He stresses repeatedly the dangers of wealth: in the story of the rich man who turned down his invitation to be a disciple, going away sad because he had many possessions (Mark 10:17-22); in his parable of the Rich Man and Lazarus, who is condemned for ignoring the poor man at his door (Luke 16:19-31); in his saying, "It is easier for a camel to pass through [the] eye of [a] needle than for one who is rich to enter the kingdom of God" (Mark 10:25); and in his parable on the Judgment of the Nations, saying that each of us will be judged on whether or not we recognize and serve Christ in those who are hungry, thirsty, a stranger, naked, ill, or in prison (Matt 25:31-46).

When the religious and political powers conspired to get rid of him, he gave himself over with a prayer: "Abba, Father, all things are possible to you. Take this cup away from me, but not what I will but what you will" (Mark 14:36).

God as Father

Jesus' characteristic word for God was Father. Behind this memory lies the Aramaic word *Abba* (dear Father), appearing in the text we just considered and used, following his example, by the early Christians in their own prayer (Rom 8:15; Gal 4:6). But Jesus' use of *Abba* was unique for a Jew of his day, none of whom would have dared address God in such intimate fashion. In fact, as we noted earlier, a Jew would not even pronounce God's sacred name. Joseph Fitzmyer, whose knowledge of Aramaic as it was used at the time of Jesus is second to none, argues that Jesus' calling God *Abba* was "exclusive to himself and otherwise unknown in pre-Christian Palestinian Jewish tradition."[1] In the word *Abba* we hear the voice of Jesus. It is the word he used in his own prayer, expressing his intimate relationship with God. We gain an insight into that relationship, as through an open window, in his parables.

The Prodigal Son (Luke 15:11-32) presents God as a loving father who, rejected by his younger son, longs for his return. When finally he sees his son returning, broken and humbled by his experience, he rushes out to welcome him. The scene is beautifully captured by Rembrandt in his famous painting. Jesus' parable of the Lost Sheep speaks of God's desire that no one be lost (Matt 18:12-14; Luke 15:4-7), while his teaching on prayer tells us that no earthly father can compare with the Father in heaven (Luke 11:9-13).

The God of Jesus is not like the patriarchal fathers of tribal Israelite or classical Roman society. When Jesus promises "houses and brothers and sisters and mothers and children and lands" for those who follow him (Mark 10:30), fathers, interestingly enough, are not mentioned; fathers "represent patriarchy, the old society in which the man alone ruled and decided."[2] For Jesus, God as Father is the model for earthly fathers, not the other way around. For example, the paarable of the Workers in the Vineyard (Matt 20:1-16), in which those hired last are paid equal to the first workers sent into the vineyard, strikes many of us as unfair. But it teaches that God is not like us, parsimoniously measuring out according to what we have earned. Instead, God like the owner of the vineyard is incredibly generous, and looks with special kindness on those unable to find work. When I hear this parable I think of the line of Latino immigrant day laborers, waiting outside a local building contractors' emporium close to our university, waiting until late in the day for someone to hire them.

Jesus taught his disciples to address God as Father in the Lord's Prayer (Matt 6:9; Luke 11:2), and Christians have followed their example down to our own time. Today however, some are uncomfortable with "Father" as a form of address for God. They see such masculine metaphors as expressions of an androcentric or "sexist" God language which reinforces the social structure of patriarchy within society and church. Both contribute to what Sandra Schneiders calls the "experienced masculinity of God," with damaging consequences, especially for

[1] Joseph A. Fitzmyer, *The Gospel According to Luke*, 2 (Garden City, NY: Doubleday, 1985) 898.

[2] Bruce Chilton and J. I. H. McDonald, *Jesus and the Ethics of the Kingdom* (Grand Rapids, MI: Eerdmans, 1987) 132.

women. Since God is not male, to speak and imagine God exclusively in masculine metaphors leads to a distorted self-image for both women and men, glorifying the masculine and reducing the female to a subordinate and derivative position. Noting that the imagination both recalls our experience and helps us to integrate and interpret it, Schneiders calls for healing our images of God, self, and world by purifying our God language of its patriarchal overtones.[3]

Tip

There are some who want to replace traditional God language, particularly our trinitarian formulas, with more inclusive, non-gendered names of God, praying for example "in the name of the Creator, the Redeemer, and the Life-giving Spirit." In June 2006 the 217th General Assembly of the Presbyterian Church in the USA (PCUSA) "received" a paper on gender-inclusive language, a step short from approving it. Seeking to find "fresh ways to speak of the mystery of the triune God," the assembly authorized church officials to allow alternative phrases for the Trinity such as "Mother, Child, and Womb," "Rock, Redeemer, Friend," or the familiar "Creator, Savior, Sanctifier," though it reserved the traditional trinitarian formula for baptism to demonstrate their ecumenical commitment.[4]

Given the Creed's confession of God as Father, what should we think of these efforts to find a less gender-specific language for God? First of all, we need to acknowledge frankly that our tradition has often failed to recognize the full equality of men and women, often at the cost of women's dignity. For example, Thomas Aquinas (1225–1274), while recognizing that woman is included in nature's intention for the work of generation and therefore is not "misbegotten," still could write as though her individual nature was "defective."

> As regards the individual nature, woman is defective and misbegotten, for the active force in the male seed tends to the production of a perfect likeness in the masculine sex; while the production of woman comes from defect in the active force or from some material indisposition, or even from some external influence; such as that of a south wind, which is moist, as the Philosopher observes (*De Gener. Animal.* iv, 2). On the other hand, as regards human nature in general, woman is not

[3] Sandra M. Schneiders, *Women and the Word: The Gender of God in the New Testament and the Spirituality of Women* (New York: Paulist Press, 1986) 16–18.

[4] See PCUSA, "The Trinity: God's Love Overflowing," pcusa.org/theologyand worship/issues/trinityfinal.

misbegotten, but is included in nature's intention as directed to the work of generation.[5]

Aquinas' view here is not specifically Christian. He is simply repeating a view present in western Mediterranean culture since Roman times that has its origins in Aristotle. Nevertheless, noninclusive language easily perpetuates this old idea that the female sex is secondary and derivative. As Mary Daly's famous phrase has it, "When God is male, then the male is God."[6]

Classical theology recognized that the transcendent, ineffable God is beyond all naming, and therefore all our God language is analogical. Because God is incomprehensible, we are dependent on analogies, metaphors, and symbols to speak meaningfully of God. What is problematic is our tendency to literalize those analogies, metaphors, or symbols, and even more, to canonize those that are masculine. It is obvious that our God language in its gender and imagery is exclusively masculine.

This over-reliance on masculine imagery is in contrast to the Scripture, which includes some feminine metaphors, in addition to the more common masculine ones. Elizabeth Johnson points to three Old Testament symbols—spirit, wisdom, and mother—with potential for the renewal of our God language.[7] Deuteronomy 32:18 says, "You forgot the God who gave you birth." Isaiah several times uses the maternal image of child birth, comparing God's love to the love of a mother for the child of her womb (Isa 49:15; cf. 66:13) or God's anguish for Israel to the pains of a woman in labor (42:14). The Wisdom tradition personifies God's wisdom as a feminine figure, *Sophia* in Greek, particularly in the book of Proverbs. Johnson observes that given that Jewish insistence on monotheism, "the idea that Sophia is Israel's God in female imagery is most reasonable."[8]

Jesus also uses the metaphor of childbirth to describe what is born of the Spirit (John 3:1-7). He compares God's love for the lost sheep to the woman who searches her house for the one lost coin (Luke 15:8-10), or God's work in bringing about the reign of God to the woman who mixes yeast into the dough for her bread (Matt 13:33). In a particularly

[5] Aquinas, *Summa Theologica*, I,92,1.

[6] Mary Daly, *Beyond God the Father* (Boston: Beacon, 1973) 19.

[7] Elizabeth A. Johnson, *She Who Is: The Mystery of God in Feminist Theological Discourse* (New York: Crossroad, 1992) 82.

[8] Ibid., 91.

beautiful passage he addresses Jerusalem, saying, "how many times I yearned to gather your children together, as a hen gathers her young under her wings" (Matt 23:37), using a tender feminine metaphor expressing God's love for Israel. Sadly, these feminine metaphors for God are rarely understood today and seldom find a place in our liturgy.

Thus it should be possible to find ways to bring some of these feminine metaphors into our liturgical and devotional language, balancing the exclusive use of the masculine. Certainly Scripture is evidence for the capacity of the feminine to image the divine, as we have seen.

But we need to move carefully when dealing with the historic symbols of the faith, such as the Creed or the church's baptismal formula. Trading functional for gendered language, as in Creator, Redeemer, and Life-giving Spirit, risks eliminating (however inadvertently) the mutual relationship between Father and Son, and thus the distinction of persons which gives us the doctrine of the Trinity. It is difficult to pray to a function. The result is a functional unitarianism that does not adequately express the Christian understanding of God. Worse, it depersonalizes God, who is not just personal, but intersubjective. In other words, relationality is at the very heart of the Christian understanding of God.

Catherine LaCugna, in her fine book *God for Us*, acknowledges that no name for God has been as ideologically abused as that of "Father." Still, she does not think using that name is always patriarchal. While she believes that calling God "Mother" may sometimes be appropriate, it remains true, she argues, that the substitution of Mother for Father "does not resolve the deep-seated problems of a unitarian theism."[9] It certainly is not traditional.

The efforts of some feminist theologians to highlight Wisdom christology rather than the traditional Son of God christology also risks describing God in unitarian terms.[10] The figure of Sophia/Wisdom in the Wisdom literature represents a feminine metaphor for God's presence and saving action in the world, applied by the early Christians to Jesus. Wisdom themes play an important christological role in Paul and the gospels, both the Synoptics and John. Jesus himself taught in the man-

[9] Catherine LaCugna, *God For Us: The Trinity and Christian Life* (HarperSanFrancisco, 1991) 18, n. 7.

[10] Elizabeth A. Johnson, "Jesus, the Wisdom of God: A Biblical Basis for Non-Androcentric Christology," *Ephemerides Theologicae Lovaniensis* 61 (1985) 335–80; Elisabeth Schüssler-Fiorenza, *Jesus: Miriam's Child, Sophia's Prophet* (New York: Continuum, 1994) esp. 131–62.

ner of the Old Testament Wisdom teachers, using their themes and their aphoristic and narrative style. The implications of Wisdom theology, both anthropological as well as christological, have yet to be fully integrated into the church's theology. If a feminine metaphor can represent Christ, it should be clear that women can also represent him. As Johnson says, "divine Sophia incarnate in Jesus addresses all persons in her call to be friends of God, and can be truly represented by any human being called in her Spirit, women as well as men."[11]

Thus the biblical Wisdom tradition helps us to move beyond exclusively masculine metaphors for God or Christ. At the same time, Brendan Byrne argues against neglecting the traditional title, Son of God, in favor of Wisdom christology. "What Wisdom Christology brings out less explicitly is the sense of God's familial involvement in the work of redemption, the sense of the cost to God in the giving up of God's own Son expressed in texts such as Rom 8:4 and 8:32." This sense of the divine vulnerability provides an important contrast to the traditional notion of God as omnipotent or all powerful.[12]

The Almighty

The *Catechism of the Catholic Church* notes that of "all the divine attributes, only God's omnipotence is named in the Creed."[13] Certainly the notion that God is all-powerful is basic to the Christian understanding of God.

The notion is ancient. According to the Old Testament, the name of the God of the fathers was El Shaddai. Though the exact meaning of Shaddai in Hebrew remains unclear, the Septuagint translation used the Greek word *pantokratōr*, "almighty" to translate it.[14] This led to the traditional but incorrect translation of Shaddai in English as "The Almighty," (Gen 17:1; Exod 6:3).

The notion of God's omnipotence is strong also in scholastic philosophy. For Aquinas, God as pure act, *ipsum esse subsistens,* is the condition

---

[11] Johnson, *She Who Is,* 165.

[12] Brendan Byrne, "Christ's Pre-existence in Pauline Soteriology," *Theological Studies* 58 (1997) 329.

[13] *Catechism of the Catholic Church,* no. 268.

[14] Pantocrator became a christological title translated as "Ruler of All," often portrayed in the domes of Orthodox churches.

for the possibility of contingent beings[15] and as such is all-powerful. He observed that God's omnipotence is limited by what is possible: "everything that does not imply a contradiction in terms, is numbered among those possible things, in respect of which God is called omnipotent."[16]

Still, this notion of divine omnipotence is a stumbling block for many today who find it difficult to believe in an omnipotent deity when there is so much tragedy and injustice in the world. Why for example, did God "permit" the holocaust of six million Jews during the Second World War in Europe's dark night under the Nazis? Could God have prevented this slaughter? Is God responsible for tsunamis or earthquakes that kill tens of thousands? Can God change the weather in answer to our prayer? Is God really all-powerful?

The Wisdom tradition in the Hebrew Scriptures wrestled with the mystery of suffering, particularly the suffering of the just. In a marvelous poetic meditation Annie Dillard suggests a different understanding of God:

> God is no more blinding people with glaucoma, or testing them with diabetes, or purifying them with spinal pain, or choreographing the seeding of tumor cells through lymph, or fiddling with chromosomes, than he is jimmying floodwaters or pitching tornados at towns. . . . The very least likely things for which God might be responsible are what insurers call "acts of God."

> Mostly, God is out of the physical loop. Or the loop is a spinning hole in his side. Simone Weil takes a notion from Rabbi Isaac Luria to acknowledge that God's hands are tied. To create, God did not extend himself but withdrew himself; he humbled and obliterated himself, and left outside himself the domain of necessity, in which he does not intervene.[17]

Dillard's concern here is an overemphasis on divine omnipotence that has the effect of making God the author of evil. Pope John Paul II once suggested something similar in a reflection on God's endowing humanity with freedom. He wrote, "In a certain sense one could say that *confronted with our human freedom, God decided to make Himself 'impotent.'*"[18]

---

[15] Thomas Aquinas, *Summa Theologica*, trans. by the Fathers of the Dominica Conference, I,3,4.

[16] Ibid., I,25,3.

[17] Annie Dillard, *For the Time Being* (New York: Alfred A. Knopf, 1999) 167–68.

[18] John Paul II, *Crossing the Threshold of Hope*, ed. Vittorio Messori (New York: Random House, 1994) 61.

The Pope's dramatic language here describes a voluntary self-limitation of the divine power, the necessary correlative to creating a world in which there is genuine freedom. In such a world, God cannot *not* respect human freedom.

We need to be careful of our language here, for we are dealing with what ultimately remains mystery. As the creator and author of life, God's power is the cause of the immeasurable universe, the creatures that inhabit it, and the beauty and value that ennoble it. All this God brings into being out of nothing and sustains. Augustine believed that God is always in control, that there is a reason for everything that happens, even if we cannot always discern it, and that God's providence will not be frustrated. Yet at the same time, some argue that the divine decision to create a world in which there is genuine spontaneity which reaches its full expression in human freedom means a necessary limitation of the divine omnipotence. If God is to create humans able to freely respond in love, God cannot overturn each decision that acts against the divine will for the good of creation.

Therefore, rather than inflating a philosophical notion of the divine omnipotence, it makes more sense to image God mysteriously at work in the world to bring about the divine purpose. The scholastic notion of God is not the only one possible. For all the limitations of American process philosophy, its authors conceive of God not as unchanging in eternal perfection, as in classical philosophy, but as responsive to the events in the world, even experiencing the world's pain and suffering. Alfred North Whitehead describes God as "the fellow sufferer who understands,"[19] shocking for some of a more traditional mindset, but perhaps not a bad way to understand God. In a similar vein, in his *Spiritual Exercises*, St. Ignatius of Loyola invites the retreatant to consider "how God works and labors for me in all creatures upon the face of the earth."[20]

Conclusion

The God Jesus called Father is the God of Israel, a God he came to know from his parents and his religious community. Thus it is a mistake to contrast the loving God of Jesus with the "wrathful" God of the Jews.

---

[19] Alfred North Whitehead, *Process and Reality: An Essay in Cosmology* (New York: Free Press, 1978) 351.

[20] Ignatius of Loyola, *The Spiritual Exercises of St. Ignatius*, ed. Louis J. Puhl (Chicago: Loyola Press, c. 1951) no. 236.

It is also deeply offensive to the Jews themselves, who experience their God as loving and compassionate.

Rich as Jesus' word *Abba* is for our understanding of God, God has many names and *Abba* remains only one metaphor. Augustine once wrote that God "is not called Father with reference to himself but only in relation to the Son; seen by himself he is simply God."[21] Christianity has been burdened by an exclusively masculine God language. Biblical metaphors such as wisdom, spirit, and mother suggest that the feminine can also image the divine. They have been employed too rarely in the Christian tradition. Still the traditional language of God as Father, Son, and Spirit safeguards the relationality that is at the heart of the divine mystery. Therefore we should honor it.

Today when more people experience God as absent rather than as omnipotent, perhaps we can gain some insight into that mystery of a God whose very "impotence" in the face of our freedom reflects the sovereign creator's love for the creature. God's ability to renounce power for persuasion, so unlike our own, is the ultimate witness to God's power, which is really benevolence rather than control. In the final analysis our philosophical and theological efforts to understand God and God's power run head-on into the mystery of the divine incomprehensibility. That mystery can be glimpsed but never dissolved. Finally, we are united to God, not by our ideas but by love.

Nowhere was this more obvious than in the becoming flesh of God in the man Jesus, the most powerful symbol of the divine renunciation of power and invulnerability. When we strive to live the *imitatio Christi*, the imitation of Christ which has always been at the heart of Christianity, calling on God as Father as Jesus did, the incomprehensible mystery begins to disclose itself as a Thou. We can then enter into relationship with God who gathers us into a sheltering embrace.

---

[21] Augustine, *Patrologia Latina* 36:845; cited by Joseph Ratzinger, *Introduction to Christianity* (San Francisco: Ignatius Press, 2004) 183.

Chapter 5

"Creator of heaven and earth"

The idea of God as creator of the heavens and the earth, the first sentence in the Bible, holds pride of place in most people's image of God. Yet the question that we continue to ask, why there is something rather than nothing, is itself a relatively modern question, as is the notion of a creation *ex nihilo* (Latin for "out of nothing").

To Aristotle's teaching on the eternity of the world, Aquinas responded that we know that the world had a beginning only from faith.[1] The Genesis creation story (Gen 1:1–2:4a) presumes that something existed before God's creative work began, for it says that "the earth was a formless wasteland, and darkness covered the abyss, while a mighty wind swept over the waters" (Gen 1:1-2). We will consider first the Genesis creation account and then some of the deeper theological implications of the doctrine of creation.

Creation in Scripture

As the Israelites settled in the land of Canaan, they encountered the universal god of the Canaanites, El or Elohim, as well as the Canaanite fertility cults, highly sexual in nature, in which the cyclical renewal of creation and its fertility were enacted. Confronted with

---

[1] Thomas Aquinas, *Summa Theologica*, trans. by the Fathers of the English Dominican Province, I,46,2.

these Mesopotamian and Canaanite creation stories, they fashioned their own, which in many ways can be seen as a demythologization of the pagan original.

The first Genesis creation account presents a magnificent picture of the God of Israel fashioning the heavens and the earth out of the primeval waters of chaos by the sheer power of the divine word (Gen 1:1–2:4a). The story concerns not the later philosophical idea of creation out of nothing, but rather the goodness of creation and the beginning of God's salvific work of bringing order, light, and life out of the primordial darkness, emptiness, and formlessness. Or more abstractly put, out of chaos, God brought cosmos. But the divine work in creation cannot be separated from God's shaping a people and preparing them to be a light to the nations (Isa 42:5-7).

That the biblical creation story is dependent on earlier Mesopotamian versions is now well known. The classic form of the Mesopotamian myth, the *Enuma Elish* epic, as we saw earlier, would have been familiar to the Israelites from the time of their exile in Babylon and probably even before. The myth celebrates the victory of the Babylonian god Marduk over chaos, personified in the myth by the monster goddess Tiamat, who represents the formless but relentlessly hostile sea. After a fierce battle, Marduk drives an evil wind into Tiamat, filling her with air, and then pierces her heart with an arrow. Using his sword he divides her in two to fashion the sky or firmament above and the earth below. Once stripped of its battling Babylonian deities, the narrative became the source for the first creation story in the book of Genesis.

When one places the Babylonian account side by side with that of Genesis, it becomes apparent that they are two different versions of the same story. Both refer to a watery chaos at the beginning of creation, though in the Babylonian original it is personified by the goddess Tiamat. The name for chaos in both accounts, *Tiamat* in *Enuma Elish*, and *Tehom*, the Deep, in Genesis, are etymologically related. Both accounts refer to the light and the alternation of day and night before the creation of the heavenly bodies later in the story. Both represent the deity as fashioning the earth by a division of the primeval waters, and both have the same order of creation: first the sky, then the dry land, the heavenly bodies, and finally the man and the woman. But notice the difference; in the Genesis account the God of Israel creates effortlessly, simply by the power of the divine word (1:1–2:4a).

Enuma Elish, Tablet IV, 135–140	Genesis 1:6-7
Then the lord paused to view her dead body, That he might divide the monster and do artful works. He split her like a shellfish into two parts: Half of her he set up and ceiled it as sky, Pulled down the bar and posted guards. He bade them to allow not her waters to escape.[2]	Then God said, "Let there be a dome in the middle of the waters, to separate one body of water from the other." And so it happened: God made the dome, and it separated the water above the dome from the water below it. God called the dome "the sky." . . . Then God said, "Let the water under the sky be gathered into a single basin, so that the dry land may appear."

One can almost sense the biblical author's scorn for the superstition of his pagan neighbors when he corrects the pagan myth, in which creation is really through procreation, or through violence. Or by pointing out that the sun, the moon, and the stars were placed in the heavens to serve humankind by marking the days and seasons, to tell time, not to be worshiped as seats for the gods. Or in teaching that the man and woman are created in God's image and likeness, not to be servants of the gods, as in the pagan story. After the work of creation is done God rests; the work is finished, unlike the Canaanite myth with its eternal cycle. Thus the Genesis creation story is already a demythologization of the pagan myth, preserving its basic structure without its sexual overtones, violence, polytheism, and superstition.

The account in Genesis 1 is unique in portraying creation simply by the power of the divine word. But there are echoes of the old cosmic battle with the forces of chaos in other parts of the Old Testament, where again the ancient monster appears. For example, Psalms 74, 89, and 93 reflect the popular Canaanite version of the story, celebrating the combat of the Canaanite god Baal with a monstrous serpent or dragon called Lotan or Leviathan, the Sea-River or sometimes Rahab. But here the God of Israel is victorious in the combat. Thus in Psalm 74:13-15 we read:

---

[2] See *The Ancient Near East: An Anthology of Texts and Pictures*, ed. James B. Pritchard (Princeton University Press, 1958) 31–39; see also Alexander Heidel, *The Babylonian Genesis: The Story of Creation* (Chicago: University of Chicago Press, 1951).

You stirred up the sea in your might;
  you smashed the heads of the dragons on the waters.
You crushed the heads of Leviathan,
  tossed him for food to the sharks.
You open up springs and torrents,
  brought dry land out of the primeval waters.

Other examples include Psalm 89:9-11, Isaiah 27:1, and Job 3:8 or 26:12-13 where Leviathan or Rahab appears. In Job 40:26 Leviathan, the terrifying serpent of the pagan myth, has become a crocodile with a rope in its nose, while in Psalm 104:26 it has lost its terrifying aspect and is merely a creature "playing" or "sporting" in God's sea.

The Genesis myth is precisely that; it is a prescientific way of giving an account of creation. Most Christians have no difficulty accepting such a story for what it teaches, that creation is the work of God's hands (Pss 8:7; 102:26), that it is good, that each human being is created in the image and likeness of God, and therefore each human life is sacred, never to be used as a means. Genesis rules out any dualistic theology which would recognize two principles, one good, spiritual, light-filled, the other evil, material, and dark.

In no way does the Genesis story contradict the theory of evolution. Nor is there need for modern religious theories such as "creation science" or "intelligent design" to save it, attempting to make the Bible a source of scientific knowledge. As a credible, well-supported hypothesis, evolution is not concerned with addressing the philosophical and theological questions of ultimate causality. It represents a careful, well-established scientific effort to explain *how* the diversity of living things came about. The theory of natural selection does not necessarily rule out God's creative, guiding presence. In 1996 Pope John Paul II acknowledged that the theory of evolution "is more than a hypothesis," though he stressed that the church teaches the uniqueness of the human person, created in the image and likeness of God.[3] Yet fundamentalist Christians continue to see evolution as an attack on the "inerrancy" of the Bible and thus as a threat to its authority. Because their understanding of truth is univocal, the Bible must be true in every sense, theologically, historically, and scientifically. They don't recognize that profound religious truths might be expressed by a myth or story.

---

[3] John Paul II, "Theories of Evolution," *Origins* (December 5, 1996).

Creatio ex Nihilo

How does theology help us to understand more deeply the biblical doctrine of creation? If Scripture teaches us of God's creative work, bringing order, life, and intelligence out of chaos, Aquinas' doctrine of contingency takes the doctrine of creation to a new level, even if Aquinas himself did not specifically link creation and contingency. The implications of his doctrine are clear. God is pure existence, self-subsisting Being. All beings apart from God have being only by participation; they cannot account for their own existence.[4] God's essence is to be; all else is a limitation of the pure dynamism of existence to be this or that or something else. Thus created reality is contingent, radically dependent on God for its existence.

Still, for Aquinas, God's gift of being to creatures was real. God works in all things as their first cause; "since the form of a thing is within the thing . . . and because in all things God Himself is properly the cause of universal being which is innermost in all things; it follows that in all things God works intimately."[5] Thus, while God is the immediate cause of all being, created beings are able to exercise an autonomous causality because they have being and form. Accidents, deaths caused by natural disasters, illness, disease, and tragedy are not caused by God, but by "secondary causality," the proper causality of a material and thus imperfect world.

But precisely as contingent being, creation, that is to say, all of us and each of us, would cease to exist without God's creative causality. Thus creation is not some divine act in the past, as many conceive it. God is creating and sustaining us in existence at this very moment. Without God's causality, or to use a more anthropomorphic metaphor, without our being held at this very instant intimately in God's heart, we would simply cease to exist.

This notion of God's continuous creation has been beautifully expressed by the psalmist, who describes the Lord as giving drink to the wild beasts of the field, watering the mountains, raising grass for the cattle and plants for our beasts of burden, bringing bread from the earth and wine to gladden our hearts:

---

[4] *Summa Theologica*, I,44,1.
[5] Ibid., I,105,5.

All of these look to you
  to give them food in due time.
When you give to them, they gather;
  when you open your hand, they are well filled.
When you hide your face, they are lost.
  When you take away their breath, they perish
  and return to the dust from which they came.
When you send forth your breath, they are created,
  and you renew the face of the earth.

(Ps 104:27-30)

The idea of God's continuous creation, exemplified in the resurrection of
Jesus and our own share in his salvation, is also present in the New Testament. It can be found in Paul's metaphor of Christ as the "last Adam"
or "the second man" (1 Cor 15:45, 47), as a "new creation" (2 Cor 5:17;
Gal 6:15), and in the idea of God's preparing a new heaven and a new
earth (Rev 21:1-5). In the final meditation in the *Spiritual Exercises* of St.
Ignatius, the "Contemplation for Obtaining Love," Ignatius invites the
retreatant "to consider how God works and labors for me in all things
created on the face of the earth—that is, behaves like one who labors—as
in the heavens, elements, plants, fruits, cattle, etc., giving them being,
preserving them, giving them vegetation and sensation, etc."[6] He is
echoing here the teaching of Aquinas.

The Nicene Creed follows the words "creator of heaven and earth" in
the Apostles' Creed with "and of all things visible and invisible." While
this may seem an unnecessary redundancy, it was added specifically
because of the dualistic Gnostic teaching, perhaps rooted in Marcion (d.
160), that the visible world of materiality, and thus the body, sexuality,
and the material world were all evil, products of a lesser deity, while
the invisible world of the spirit was good. The effect of this addition to
the Nicene was to affirm that all creation, whether visible or invisible,
was the work of God. Thus in an age in which virginity was often seen
as the higher way of life and marriage condemned, especially in the
teaching of the Gnostics, Christianity sanctified marriage, sexuality,
and children. While the church has never completely freed itself from
the remnants of this dualism, the Creed's affirmation is an important
one, recognizing the goodness of our embodied existence. Indeed, the

---

[6] Ignatius of Loyola, *The Spiritual Exercises of St. Ignatius*, ed. Louis J. Puhl (Chicago:
Loyola Press, c. 1951) no. 236.

doctrine of the Incarnation teaches us that the human becomes the embodiment of the divine.

Conclusion

Traditional theology has seen God's creative work as an expression of the divine omnipotence. Yet today this is too often taken for granted. Many have lost sight of the world of our experience as God's work and ourselves as radically contingent, owing our very existence to a mysterious Other who continues to sustain us. To speak of God as creator of all that is seen and unseen is to confess that the world does not explain itself. The very word "creation" suggests intelligence, a benevolent artisan rather than the Gnostic Demiurge, a lesser deity responsible for the corrupt if not evil world of matter from which the enlightened sought release. Unlike Gnosticism, even in its Christian expressions, orthodox Christianity values the created order, including our bodies, our sexuality, and our human relationships. Elaine Pagels, one of the premiere scholars of Gnosticism, saw this clearly; she writes, "[o]rthodox Christians were concerned—far more than Gnostics—with their relationships with other people."[7] Indeed God's gift of salvation is inseparable from our relationships with others.

If contemporary expressions of Gnosticism promise salvation for a spiritual elite who fashion their own "spirituality," independent of creed, cult, and church, orthodox Christianity emphasizes that our salvation is intrinsically related to our real relationships in the world. One cannot be a Christian by oneself, without the Christian community.

Some scholars have seen creation as a divine *kenosis*, a self-emptying, limiting the divine omnipotence by bringing into existence intelligent beings endowed with a freedom that God must respect. British physicist and Anglican priest John Polkinghorne tries to steer a middle course between an all-powerful God understood as puppet master of the universe and the detached God of deism. He describes creation as involving "a voluntary limitation, not only of divine power in allowing the other to be, but also of divine knowledge in allowing the future to be open."[8] While a free future doesn't necessarily exclude divine foreknowledge,

---

[7] Elaine Pagels, *The Gnostic Gospels* (New York: Random House, 1989) 146.

[8] "Chaos Theory and Divine Action," in *Religion and Science: History, Method, Dialogue*, ed. W. Mark Richardson and Wesley J. Wildman (New York: Routledge, 1996) 250.

these different ways of conceiving the divine agency in creation can enrich our attempt to understand something of the mystery of God who remains incomprehensible.

Might it also be possible to see in creation a maternal sharing of God's own being, just as a mother gives life to the child of her womb out of the substance of her own body? This is not to suggest that we adopt goddess language, or to deny the real distinction between God and created reality. But it does invite us to explore the suitability of feminine metaphors for God, just as we have traditionally used masculine ones.

Jesus Christ

Chapter 6

"I believe in Jesus Christ, his only Son, our Lord."

The second part of the Apostles' Creed confesses faith in Jesus Christ, the only Son of God. The longest part of the Creed, it first proclaims Jesus' relationship to God, using three biblical titles: Jesus is the Christ of Israel, the only Son of God, confessed as Lord by those who have been baptized. The second and longer part summarizes the story of his birth of the Virgin Mary, crucifixion, death, descent into hell, resurrection, ascension to glory, and expected coming again in judgment, most of which is told in the gospel narratives. We will consider first what is affirmed about Jesus in the titles, thus the church's christology. In the next chapter, we will look more carefully at the Jesus story, presented only schematically here.

Jesus the Christ

Christians sometimes differ as to how they talk to or about Jesus. Evangelicals often use his personal name, Jesus. Catholics and mainstream Protestant Christians often refer to him as Christ, in part because the title refers to the post-Easter, glorified Jesus, and perhaps in part because they are less comfortable with a language that seems overly personal. The disciples did not immediately confess Jesus as messiah, Lord, or Son of God; their understanding of his true identity developed gradually.

The name Jesus, *Yeshua* in Aramaic, very common in New Testament times, means "Yahweh is salvation" (cf. Matt 1:21). The English word

Christ comes from the Greek *Christos*, literally "anointed," used in the
Septuagint to translate the Hebrew *mashiah*, "anointed one." *Christos* is
derived from the same Greek root as the word "chrism," the holy oil
used in the sacraments. To call Jesus the Christ then is to identify him
as the messiah or anointed of Israel. It is a royal title.

While there is no unified concept of the messiah in the Old Testament,
a trajectory of images contributed to its becoming an important expression of Jewish hope still strong in the time of Jesus. Its roots lie in the so-
called "Oracle of Nathan." Moved by David's piety, the prophet Nathan
promised that God would raise up for David an heir who would inherit
an everlasting kingdom; God would be a father to him and he would be a
son to God (2 Sam 7:11-14; cf. Ps 89:20-38). While the passage referred to
David's son Solomon (1 Chr 17:11-14; 22:9-10), in the subsequent tradition
the idea developed that God's covenant with Israel would be fulfilled
through the house and family of David, particularly through an anointed
descendant. Some of the psalms repeat the idea that the king is begotten
by God (Ps 110:3; cf. 89:27) and can be called God's son (Ps 2:7). "Son of
God" thus becomes another way of saying Son of David.

The image of a future Davidic king or messiah as an agent of God's
salvation appears in the psalms and prophets; he will judge the nations
(Ps 110), shepherd them (Ps 2), bring light to those who walk in darkness (Isa 9:1-5), "govern wisely" (Jer 23:5), and bring justice to the poor,
an important characteristic of the messianic age (Isa 11:1-11). Sometimes
the idea is broadened, with God's agency working through the people,
Israel, so that the reign of Yahweh might embrace all peoples (Isa 2:1-4;
Mic 4:1-2; Pss 47; 96–100).

The Jesus of history did not talk much about himself. The focus of
his preaching was that God's kingdom or reign was at hand, though its
coming could not be separated from his ministry or his person. Peter's
confession of Jesus as the messiah, which plays a pivotal role in the
gospel narratives, suggests that some at least of Jesus' contemporaries
interpreted his ministry in messianic terms (Mark 8:29). Jesus healed
the sick, reached out to the troubled and the marginal, proclaimed that
sins were forgiven and the poor blessed. His practice of table fellowship,
evoking the criticism that he was "a friend of tax collectors and sinners"
(Matt 11:19), showed that no one was excluded from God's reign. To
encounter Jesus was to encounter God's reign. In gathering disciples,
his movement sought to reconstitute Israel as the community of salvation, building his movement around "the twelve" (Mark 3:13-19), whose
appointment was highly symbolic.

Certainly the early Jewish Christians saw his ministry as fulfilling the promise of the messianic age of salvation (Luke 7:22). Thus it was natural that they saw him as the messiah. So closely has the title messiah or Christ been associated with Jesus that it is often used as though the two words constituted his name, Jesus Christ (Matt 1:1; John 1:17). And indeed that usage in the church is very ancient, perhaps even earlier than Paul, who prefers to say Christ Jesus, though sometimes he refers to Jesus simply as Christ (Rom 8:9, 10; 1 Cor 10:4). Perhaps Paul's most characteristic expression for the mystery of salvation is the phrase "in Christ." He uses it to express God's work of salvation accomplished through Christ Jesus (Rom 3:24; 2 Cor 2:14; 1 Thess 5:18), that our new life united us to Christ (Rom 6:11; 8:2; 1 Cor 15:22), and to describe our life in the church as an incorporation into Christ (Rom 8:1; 1 Cor 4:15; 15:19; Gal 3:28). Indeed, being in the church *is* to be in Christ. One cannot be in Christ without being in his body (1 Cor 12:13).

His Only Son

The earliest version of the Apostles' Creed in Hippolytus' *Apostolic Tradition* asks simply, do you believe in Christ Jesus, the Son of God? Referring to Jesus as God's "only son" is to use a biblical metaphor that has undergone a considerable development, even metamorphosis. In the Old Testament the title "son of God" has a variety of meanings or usages. It could refer to the expected "son of David," the royal successor who God had promised to adopt (2 Sam 7:14; Ps 89:27), as we have seen. "Son of God" was used also for the just man in the Wisdom tradition (Sir 4:10; Wisdom 2:16-20), for angels (Job 1:6; 2:1), and sometimes for the people of Israel collectively (Exod 4:22; Deut 14:1). The title Son of God was also used in other eastern religions for kings and wonder workers. None of these have the implication of divinity, nor do all of the appearances of this title in the New Testament. But by the later New Testament period "Son of God" is becoming a root metaphor for Jesus which, in drawing together various ways of expressing the meaning of Jesus, takes on the sense in which we understand it today. Jesus is God's Son; he shares in God's nature.

While the title "son" was used very early for Jesus, perhaps on the basis of his resurrection which was seen by the early Christians as the moment of his appointment to divine sonship (Rom 1:3-4), there is considerable evidence that Jesus himself understood his relationship to God in filial terms. The Q tradition, used by both Matthew and Luke, suggests that he saw himself as "son" in a unique sense (Cf. Matt 11:27; Luke

10:22). He speaks of himself as "son" and God as "Father," using the Aramaic *Abba*, as we have seen. As Pope Benedict has written, "Jesus' prayer is the true origin of the term 'the Son.'"[1] The gospel writers develop this theme. The story of the virginal conception of Jesus in both Matthew and Luke suggests that Jesus is God's Son in a unique way, conceived not by normal sexual relations but through the power of the Holy Spirit (Luke 1:35; Matt 1:18-25).[2] The story tells us that Jesus' real father was God. Thus the title Son of God plays an important role in the Gospels of Mark and Matthew and throughout the Gospel of John. John is the only New Testament author to use the expression "only son" (*monogenes*, literally only begotten; John 1:14, 18; 3:16, 18; 1 John 4:9). An early Christian creed confessed Jesus as the Son of God (1 John 4:15; cf. 2:23; Heb 4:14; and Acts 8:37, a verse missing in some early manuscripts).

The New Testament includes a variety of christological traditions that identify Jesus with God. The Wisdom tradition, with its personification of Wisdom (Prov 1, 8, 9; Sir 24; Wis 7–9; Bar 3:9–4:4) coming forth from God (Sir 24:3; Prov 8:22-23), being involved in creation (Prov 8:25-31; Sir 1:4; Wis 7:22; 9:9), and having a mission to God's people (Wis 6:12-16; 9:10-18; 10-12) seems to have played an important role in attributing preexistence to Jesus, perhaps as early as Paul. In his letter to the Philippians (ca. 54), Paul says, "though he was in the form of God, [he], did not regard equality with God something to be grasped. Rather, he emptied himself, taking the form of a slave, coming in human likeness; and found human in appearance" (Phil 2:6-7; cf. 2 Cor 8:9). While this understanding of the text has been disputed, Roger Haight acknowledges that an increasing number of scholars see it as affirming Christ's preexistence.[3]

The Gospel of John has a very high christology; it speaks in the Prologue of Jesus as the eternal Word become flesh, the foundation for the doctrine of the Incarnation. It also uses repeatedly the divine formula "I AM," the Greek *ego eimi*, used in the Septuagint to translate the Hebrew revelatory formula "I am Yahweh" (Exod 6:7); and culminates with Thomas' great confession of faith before the risen Jesus as "My Lord and my God" (John 20:28). This represents the clearest example in the New Testament where the word "God" is predicated of Jesus, though there are others (cf. Heb 1:8-9).

---

[1] Joseph Ratzinger/Pope Benedict XVI, *Jesus of Nazareth* (New York: Doubleday, 2007).

[2] See Thomas P. Rausch, *Who Is Jesus? An Introduction to Christology* (Collegeville, MN: Liturgical Press, 2003) 131–37.

[3] Cf. Roger Haight, *Jesus Symbol of God* (Maryknoll, NY: Orbis Press, 1999) 169.

Our Lord

Perhaps the most significant christological title for the earliest Jewish Christians was Lord (*Mari* or *Maran* in Aramaic, *Kyrios* in Greek), for it was a title also used for God.[4] The titles *kyrios* and the feminine *kyria* were used of pagan gods and goddesses. Similarly, the Roman emperor was called *kyrios*, not just for his sovereignty, but also with intimations of divinity. But *kyrios* would have had special meaning for the Jews. First of all, they were strict monotheists. Secondly, the Septuagint translators had used *kyrios* to translate the *tetragrammaton*, the four consonants that stood for the sacred name Yahweh in the Hebrew Scriptures. In the New Testament Lord is used frequently for God. But it is also one of the most common titles for Jesus, evidenced by one of the earliest New Testament confessions of faith: "No one can say, 'Jesus is Lord,' except by the holy Spirit" (1 Cor 12:3; cf. Phil 2:11; 1 Cor 8:6; 2 Cor 4:5; Rom 10:9; Col 2:6). Jews familiar with the Septuagint would not have used this title without knowing its significance.

According to Joseph Fitzmyer, Paul inherited the title "Lord" for the risen Christ from the Palestinian Jewish community at Jerusalem.[5] Some of the earliest communities made Jesus the object of prayer, invoking him as Lord (cf. 1 Cor 1:2). Their prayer is preserved in both the Aramaic formula *Marana tha*, "O Lord, come" (1 Cor 16:22) and in Greek, "Come, Lord Jesus" (Rev 22:20). Though the early Christians continued to invoke God as "Lord," one of the most common ways of addressing Jesus was the expression found later in the Nicene Creed, "Lord Jesus Christ" (Rom 13:14; Col 1:3; Jas 1:1; 1 Pet 1:3). The phrase Lord Jesus Christ appears most often in blessings (Eph 1:2; Phil 1:2; 1 Thess 1:1), exhortations (Eph 5:20), and doxologies (2 Thess 1:12; 1 Pet 1:3), suggesting a liturgical use. One blessing, trinitarian in form, is used in our liturgy to this day: "The grace of the Lord Jesus Christ and the love of God and the fellowship of the holy Spirit be with all of you" (2 Cor 13:13). This usage, confessing Jesus, invoking him in prayer, greeting or blessing others in his name witnesses to the belief of the earliest Christians that Jesus, raised from the dead, "exalted at the right hand of God" (Acts 2:33), and glorified (John 17:5), now shares fully in the life of God.

---

[4] See Joseph A. Fitzmyer, "*Kyrios* and *Maranatha* and Their Aramaic Background," *To Advance the Gospel: New Testament Studies* (New York: Crossroad, 1981) 222.

[5] Joseph A. Fitzmyer, "Pauline Theology" in the *New Jerome Biblical Commentary*, ed. Raymond W. Brown, Joseph A. Fitzmyer, and Roland Murphy (Englewood Cliffs, NJ: Prentice Hall, 1990) 82:53.

2)

The Nicene Interpretation

The Nicene-Constantinopolitan Creed includes a long interpretation of the church's christological faith that reflects third- and fourth-century disputes over the nature of Jesus.

> We believe in one Lord, Jesus Christ,
> the only Son of God,
> eternally begotten of the Father,
> God from God, Light from Light,
> true God from true God,
> begotten, not made,
> one in Being with the Father.
> Through him all things were made.
> For us men and for our salvation,
> he came down from heaven:

Some of the language here is mythic (came down from heaven), some biblical (Lord, Christ, only Son of God, through him all things were made), some philosophical (one in being with, from the Greek, *homoousios*; Latin, *consubstantalis*).

The background to the disputes that led to this complex formula for asserting Jesus' identity is itself complex. As the church expanded beyond its Jewish roots into the Greco-Roman world, it became of necessity involved in a dialogue with culture such as the church faces in every age, if it is to intelligibly proclaim the Gospel that has been entrusted to it. Greco-Roman culture was Hellenistic. Its language was very different from the largely mythopoetic language of the Bible; it was more philosophical, abstract, dualistic, using the universal, ontological concepts of Hellenistic philosophy.

One in Being with the Father

In this context, the church struggled to combine its monotheistic faith in God with its New Testament faith in Jesus' divine Sonship. And it had to do this while preserving Christ's unity as one person, without dividing him into two different beings. As it began using the philosophical language of the day, it had to guard its faith against certain religious expressions of that philosophical worldview. Gnosticism shared the dualistic Greek prejudice against the corruptible world of materiality. Privileging the unique, indivisible divine spirit, it tended to reduce the Johannine Logos or Word to a lesser emanation from God. Salvation was not a matter of forgiveness of sins and incorporation into Christ, but rather meant escaping the entanglements of bodily existence by having the right kind of knowledge (*gnosis*). Docetism, a form of Gnosticism, denied that the divine Word had truly taken on flesh, with all the nasty implications of corruptible materiality, and thus asserted that Jesus only "seemed to die" (*dokeō* in Greek means "to seem"). They denied the significance of our embodied existence, the salvific character of the death of Jesus, and the church's belief "that the Eucharist is really the flesh of our Savior Jesus Christ."[6]

The church's effort to express the mystery of the divine Sonship of Jesus was complicated by the struggle between two competing theological schools. The catechetical school of Alexandria, founded in 195 by Clement of Alexandria, was characterized by a reverence for the transcendence and unity of God. Its doctrine, characterized as a Word-Flesh christology, stressed that the Logos has in some way "entered into" or become "attached" to the flesh of Jesus, though it was not as clear on the full humanity of Jesus as a man. The other school, at Antioch, dates from the second half of the third century. The Antiochean theologians used the language of two natures to emphasize the full humanity of Jesus; their doctrine has been characterized as a Word-Man christology. One sees a similar polarity today between some liberal christologies that stress the full humanity of Jesus but deny his divinity, and others that so emphasize his divinity that they effectively deny that he was really as human as we are (though without sin).

A first step towards securing the church's doctrine of Jesus was taken by the Council of Nicaea, called by the Emperor Constantine in 325 in response to the furor created by the heresy known as Arianism. About 318 Arius (b. 256), a priest of Alexandria, using Colossians 1:15 and other texts, began teaching that the Logos or Word had a beginning in time, coining the catchy slogan, "there was a time when he was not." Hence for Arius Jesus was a creature. His theology can be seen as a Hellenizing of Christian doctrine, turning the Logos into a mediator between the unchanging God and the world of multiplicity and change. In response, the 318 bishops who gathered at Nicaea hammered out a confession of faith or creed which affirmed the divinity of Jesus and his equality or consubstantiality with the Father.

---

[6] Cf., Ignatius of Antioch (d. 110), *To the Smyrnaens*, no. 6.

The bishops' concern, evident from the council's canons, was to affirm the church's belief in the divinity of Jesus. First, it condemned Arius' teaching that the Son of God had a beginning in time, was a creature, or was subject to change or alteration. Second, using rather awkward language that was later modified at Ephesus, it three times affirmed that the Son of God was begotten, rather than made; in other words, the Son was not created but has his eternal origin in the Father. Third, it affirmed that the Son of God was "one in being [*homoousios*] with the Father." Most of the imagery here is biblical. "Only begotten," used twice in John's gospel (1:14; 3:16), though not always clear in our English translations, stressed Jesus' unique relationship to the Father (John 1:1). Light is a rich metaphor for God, particularly common in John's gospel. The Son's role in creation is mentioned in three independent traditions, John (1:3), Paul (1 Cor 8:6; Col 1:16), and Hebrews (1:2). The term in our translation here, "one in being with" or "consubstantial" introduces an unfamiliar philosophical term into the language of the Creed to assert the ontological unity of Jesus and the Father.

The bishops at Nicaea had safeguarded belief in the divinity of the Son, making it clear that it was God who was working our salvation in the person of Jesus. Nicaea's Creed was simplified somewhat by Constantinople I in 381, which also added an article confessing belief in the divinity of the Holy Spirit. But without providing a careful definition of what exactly it meant by *homoousios*, considerable controversy continued over the humanity of Jesus. After several additional councils, finally a gathering of six hundred bishops (or five hundred, depending on the source) meeting at the Council of Chalcedon in 451 agreed upon a solemn definition, using the Antiochian two-nature language. Jesus was "truly God and truly man, of a rational soul and a body; consubstantial with the Father as regards his divinity, and the same consubstantial with us as regards his humanity, like us in all things but sin" (DS 301).

Of course how Jesus could be fully human and fully divine has occasioned endless speculation. Contemporary theological anthropology, for example, that of Karl Rahner, speaks of the structure of our being as openness to transcendence which is already grasped (pre-apprehended) unthematically or pre-conceptually, in the sense that we can experience something without knowing it clearly and distinctly.[7] In a real sense, the

---

[7] Karl Rahner, *Foundations of Christian Faith; An Introduction to the Idea of Christianity* (New York: Seabury Press, 1978) esp. 31–39.

openness towards the divine which is the structure of every human being is so perfectly realized in the man Jesus that his union with the one he called Abba is absolute and full. In his life and ministry Jesus' relation to God was the deepest center of his own identity. He is what we are called to be. As man, Jesus' union with God makes the two one. As divine Word, the perfect image of the Father, he is the Word become flesh.

For our Salvation

In reporting on his massive work on christology, Edward Schillebeeckx makes an important observation about what the first disciples experienced through their encounter with Jesus. His remark helps us to understand in more experiential terms what salvation in Christ means.

> Christianity is not a message which has to be believed, but an experience of faith which becomes a message, and as an explicit message seeks to offer a new possibility of life-experience to others who hear it from within their own experience of life.[8]

What was the experience of the first disciples? Remember that they had abandoned Jesus to his fate, leaving him to face it alone, save for some of the women who were present to the end. Their Easter experience was one of forgiveness and reconciliation, joy in his presence, and peace. As they came to recognize Jesus present at their gatherings in a new way, "in the Spirit," they understood themselves as sent or missioned to bring this good news to others. In the appendix to the Fourth Gospel, the risen Jesus not only welcomes Peter who had denied him, but commissions him as pastor of his flock (John 21:15-17).

The New Testament frequently uses the word salvation (*sōtēria*) to describe the new life the disciples experienced from God in Christ. The term needs to be understood against the Old Testament background; the concept of salvation derives from the Hebrew root YŠ, which has the connotation of space, freedom, and security gained by removing restrictions. It means being rescued, set free, made whole.

Luke Timothy Johnson presents a detailed analysis of how salvation was understood by the early Christians, based on the writings of the New Testament. While we can only summarize here, he makes it clear that this salvation is not primarily something hoped for, but something

---

[8] Edward Schillebeeckx, *Interim Report on the Books Jesus and Christ* (New York: Crossroad, 1982) 50.

they had already experienced. Thus, they speak of the charge to witness to the ends of the earth and make disciples of all nations. They speak of freedom, from cosmic powers, from oppressive law, and from sin and death. Associated with freedom are the terms deliverance, redemption, liberation, and salvation. From a more positive perspective, they claimed an experience of power or empowerment, sometimes expressed as authority (*exousia*), energy (*energeia*), and power (*dynamis*), expressed both in "signs and wonders" and in spiritual transformation. Three terms occur repeatedly in relation to this experience of power: eternal life, forgiveness of sins, and Holy Spirit.[9]

It was this experience of new life and the power of the Spirit that led the early Christians to shift the focus of their preaching from the kingdom of God to Jesus himself. They grasped implicitly the intrinsic connection between Jesus and his message. In Paul's words: "the kingdom of God is not a matter of food and drink, but of righteousness, peace, and joy in the holy Spirit" (Rom 14:17). Origen spoke of Jesus as the "kingdom in person," a theme elaborated by Joseph Ratzinger:

> Jesus is the Kingdom, not simply by virtue of his physical presence but through the Holy Spirit's radiant power flowing forth from him. In his Spirit-filled activity, smashing the demonic enslavement of man, the Kingdom of God becomes reality, God taking the government of this world into his own hands. . . . Jesus' actions, words, sufferings break the power of that alienation which lies so heavily on human life. In liberating people, they establish God's Kingdom. Jesus *is* that Kingdom since through him the Spirit of God acts in the world.[10]

While there is a fulfillment to our salvation that will only be realized in God's future, we should experience salvation in Christ as empowering and transforming us right now. Life in the Spirit is a present reality. The German philosopher Friedrich Nietzsche once observed astutely, "Christians should look more redeemed." One of the reasons that Pentecostal Christianity is growing so rapidly today is that Pentecostals focus on the power of the Holy Spirit to change lives. Many who become Pentecostal

---

[9] See Luke Timothy Johnson, *The Creed: What Christians Believe and Why It Matters* (New York: Doubleday, 2003) 142–50.

[10] Joseph Ratzinger, *Eschatology: Death and Eternal Life*, trans. ed. Aidan Nichols (Washington, DC: The Catholic University of America Press, 1988) 34–35; Origen PG13, 1197B.

have stories of being freed from depression, alcoholism, drug addiction, or marital infidelity. Life in the Spirit should indeed be different!

Of course, we all know men and women whose lives are living testimony to the Spirit's presence, enabling their discipleship. There are obvious examples like Mother Teresa, Archbishop Oscar Romero, Dorothy Day, and Brother Roger of Taizé. But there are also countless men and women who strive to be loving spouses, good parents, powerful witnesses to their faith; there are those who have devoted their energies to the service of the disadvantaged, chosen simple lifestyles for careers that are also ministries or vocations, or who live lives of joy and generosity in the midst of poverty because they are believers.

While salvation in Christ should never be turned into a this-worldly ideology, it does have important implications for our personal and social relations in this world. God's salvation in Christ is "political" in the sense that it involves our real, historical existence, including our existence in community both ecclesial and civil. There is a liberating dimension to our life in Christ, as it frees us from sin and enables us to live in communion with one another. Without denying that our ultimate destiny lies beyond this world or that the kingdom of God is ultimately God's work, theologies of liberation are concerned to emphasize the social implications of the Gospel. God works through us; or as the old Catholic principle holds, grace builds on nature. Spiritualities of liberation reject any separation between theology and spirituality. They argue that just as a genuine spirituality must be focused on the cross of Jesus, it cannot ignore the crucified peoples of the world today where Christ continues to suffer.[11]

With the Nicene-Constantinopolitan Creed the parameters for the church's christology were dogmatically established; it remains the norm for its christological faith.

Conclusion

The second article of the Apostles' Creed confesses our belief in "Jesus Christ, [God's] only Son, Our Lord." The three titles, Christ, Son, and Lord are rich in christological meaning. The title "Christ" identifies Jesus as the messiah of Israel, the one through whom God's promised salvation has come.

---

[11] See for example, Jon Sobrino, *The Principle of Mercy: Taking the Crucified People from the Cross* (Maryknoll, NY: Orbis Press, 1994).

"Son of God" uses the root metaphor of the divine Sonship, pulling together a number of New Testament traditions testifying to the growing recognition of the divinity of Jesus in the various New Testament communities. The Nicene-Constantinopolitan Creed offers another, more developed commentary, forged in the controversies of the first four centuries and reaching its full expression at the Council of Chalcedon.

The title "Lord," a divine title with roots in the Old Testament, expresses Christ's dominion over creation and the lives of those who hear his call to discipleship. To be a Christian means to accept Jesus, to place him first, pledging him love and obedience, following him as "the way and the truth and the life" (John 14:6). Through the centuries martyrs have given their lives, rather than compromise their commitment to the Lordship of Jesus.

Some object in principle to accepting the lordship of another, or "heteronomy." The concept is offensive for them, for it means that the self is no longer autonomous or sovereign. Some feminist theologians have objected to the language of Lordship of Jesus, seeing in it another expression of a patriarchy which contributes to the oppression of women. Kilian McDonnell sees this as a problematic aspect of some contemporary feminist christologies, since christology necessarily involves heteronomy and Jesus himself was submissive to the Father. He gratefully acknowledges the contributions feminist theologians have made to Mariology. But he asks: "Should it not be possible to reject patriarchy and still embrace some form of heteronomy in Mariology and beyond? Or is heteronomy, like patriarchy, beyond redemption."[12]

Others today seem to reject the Lordship of Jesus in practice, for it means a decentering of the self. Such people make faith, belief, and practice all matters of personal choice. Their belief systems are self-constructed. Without any mediating authority, whether Scripture, church, or Creed, they are accountable to no one or no thing external to the self. Even if they claim to be Christian, such spiritual autonomy leaves little room for the one Christians confess as our Lord Jesus Christ, the one at whose name "every knee should bend, of those in heaven and on earth and under the earth" (Phil 3:10). This is the Jesus who, identified with a given historical people, gathered a community in his name and continues to animate it with his Spirit.

---

[12] See Kilian McDonnell, "Feminist Mariologies: Heteronomy / Subordination and the Scandal of Christology," *Theological Studies* 66, no. 3 (September 2005) 565.

There is a profound social dimension to confessing Jesus as Lord. It means having no other god, and at the same time, renouncing any lordship over others. It means asking to be received under his standard, as St. Ignatius instructs the retreatant in his Meditation on the Two Standards in his *Spiritual Exercises*.[13] In Latin America this has often been understood as involving a spirituality of liberation which may involve martyrdom. It means imitating Jesus, who "did not come to be served but to serve and to give his life as a ransom for many" (Mark 10:45). It means following his commandment: "As I have loved you, so you also should love one another" (John 13:34).

[13] Ignatius of Loyola, *The Spiritual Exercises of St. Ignatius*, ed. Louis J. Puhl (Chicago: Loyola Press, c. 1951) no. 147.

Chapter 7

"He was conceived by the power of the Holy Spirit and born of the Virgin Mary."

The next section of the Creed turns to the main events in the life of Jesus. The stark narrative, "conceived by the power of the Holy Spirit, born of the Virgin Mary, suffered under Pontius Pilate, was crucified, died, and was buried," tells the story of his life in a few brief words. But it also underlines the corporeal, embodied, human nature of Jesus.

The context for the Creed's concern here was the Docetist heresy, a species of Gnosticism which with its Greek distaste for the world of corruptible materiality, denied that the divine Word had truly taken on flesh (*sarx*). As we have seen, Docetism taught that Jesus only seemed to be human, and therefore did not really suffer or die. In this chapter we will consider the Creed's teaching on the virgin birth. Even though it is not really consistent with the early church's polemic against Docetism, it is essential to understanding what we profess here in the Creed. In the next chapter we will focus on the death of Jesus.

The Birth of Jesus

Though critical scholarship can recover some of the history that lies behind the gospels, they are not to be considered literal, historical accounts of the Jesus story, his birth, life, and, death. They represent early Christian preaching (Greek: *euangélion*, "good news"), not history in our modern sense. Thus Matthew and Luke testify to the unique significance of Jesus' birth by including elaborate genealogies, infancy narratives, and in Luke's case, a wonderful story about Jesus as a boy (Luke 2:41-52).

The two genealogies are quite different. Matthew's (1:2-16) is confined to Israel; it traces Jesus' lineage from Abraham to Joseph, the putative husband of Mary, and includes four women, Tamar, Rahab, Ruth, and Bathsheba, identified only as the mother of Solomon. Interestingly, Jesus' family tree, like our own, includes both saints and sinners. Of the four women mentioned, Tamar tricked her father-in-law into sleeping with her so that she might have a child (Gen 38), Rahab was a Canaanite prostitute from Jericho who sheltered the spies sent by Joshua (Josh 2), Ruth, a Moabite woman remembered for her filial piety, became the great-grandmother of David (Ruth 4:17), and Bathsheba was seduced by David, who later arranged the death of her husband (2 Sam 11). Luke's genealogy (3:23-38) is more universal; it begins with Joseph and moves backwards to Adam. In the period from David to Joseph, Matthew and Luke have only two names in common, Zerubbabel and Shealtiel.

While the genealogies themselves are not considered historical, few would dispute that Jesus was of Davidic lineage, something affirmed frequently in the New Testament. An early creedal formula in Paul's letter to the Romans identifies Jesus as "descended from David according to the flesh" (Rom 1:3). Another introduces a summary of Paul's gospel in Second Timothy, affirming that Jesus is "of the seed of David" (2 Tim 2:8). Jesus would have been recognized as being of Davidic descent, whether or not Joseph was his real father, since according to the Jewish legal tradition adoptive paternity was sufficient for all the rights of heredity.

The infancy narratives—the stories surrounding Jesus' birth, the coming of the magi, the slaughter of the innocents and flight into Egypt in Matthew as well as Luke's careful paralleling of the stories of the conception and birth of John the Baptist and Jesus, and the adoration of the shepherds—are considered to be theological affirmations of Jesus' divine origin, messianic role, and universal significance.[1] Thus Matthew presents him as Son of Abraham and Emmanuel (Matt 1:18-25), Son of David (Matt 2:1-12), and a new Moses (Matt 2:13-15). Luke proclaims Jesus as Son of David (Luke 1:32-33) and Son of God (Luke 1:35). Many commentators consider these infancy stories a type of Christian midrash, a homiletic interpretation of the Old Testament by way of storytelling. Luke adds the story of the twelve-year-old Jesus teaching the elders in the Temple (Luke 2:52). While similar to the stories about the boyhood of Jesus in the

---

[1] See Raymond E. Brown, *The Birth of the Messiah: A Commentary on the Infancy Narratives in the Gospels of Matthew and Luke* (New York: Doubleday, 1993).

apocryphal gospels, no doubt the work of pious imagination, it serves to justify Jesus' authority and attest again that God is his Father.

Born of the Virgin Mary

The New Testament does not offer us much information of what we might call the Mary of history.[2] Paul tells us only that "God sent his Son, born of a woman, born under the law" (Gal 4:4). Mark seems to include Mary among the members of Jesus' family who thought him to be "out of his mind" when he began preaching (Mark 3:21, 31-35). John places the "mother of Jesus" in the story of the wedding at Cana (John 2:1-11) and beneath the cross where she becomes the mother of the disciples (19:26), but he never refers to her by name. Acts 1:14 puts "Mary the mother of Jesus, and his brothers" with the eleven and some other women in the upper room in the days before Pentecost.

Both Matthew and Luke report the virginal conception of Jesus, though the story is not in Mark, their principal source. Their accounts differ, suggesting that an earlier version lies behind them. Again, they represent a way of teaching that God is the real Father of Jesus (Matt 1:18-21/Luke 1:34–35), not in a biological sense, as in the pagan stories of divine conception, but by the creative power of the Holy Spirit. This tradition of the virginal conception of Jesus is the only infancy material that has become part of the official teaching of the church.

The Apocryphal gospels of the second and third centuries show considerable interest in Mary. Though they may reflect early traditions, they come from schismatic or heretical groups. *The Ascension of Isaiah* suggests that the birth of Jesus came about miraculously. *The Odes of Solomon* describes Mary as a powerful "mother with many mercies" who brought forth Jesus without pain. *The Protoevangelium* or *Gospel of James*, from the middle of the second century, is rich in material that became part of the later tradition, including the names of Joachim and Anna as the parents of Mary and stories of her birth, presentation in the Temple, and betrothal to Joseph, often with marvelous details. This apocryphal work seems to have been the first to assert the perpetual virginity of Mary, explaining the "brothers and sisters" of Jesus mentioned in the gospels as children of Joseph by a previous marriage. The *Assumption of the Virgin* (late fourth

[2] See the ecumenical study, *Mary in the New Testament*, ed. Raymond E. Brown, Karl P. Donfried, and Joseph A. Fitzmyer (Philadelphia/New York: Fortress Press/ Paulist Press, 1978).

century?) which circulated widely in Greek, Latin, Syriac, Coptic, and Arabic versions tells the story of Mary's death and assumption into heaven. Though these apocryphal works were never accepted by the church, the stories we have been considering reflect attempts to fill in details about the life of Jesus and Mary not found in the canonical gospels.

What is interesting is that fathers of the church continue to mention the virginity of Mary from the early second century on, though in much more sober terms, even though this denial of Jesus' birth through normal biological generation does not seem to have been a particularly effective argument for their ongoing polemic against the Docetists who denied the humanity of Jesus. Thus Ignatius of Antioch (d. 110) refers to the virginity of Mary, as does Justin Martyr (d. 165) and Irenaeus of Lyons (d. 200). The interrogatory creed of Hippolytus (ca. 215) asks, "Do you believe in Christ Jesus, the Son of God, Who was begotten by the Holy Spirit from the Virgin Mary?" With the Council of Constantinople (381) "born of the virgin Mary" became part of the Creed, with the further addition, "and became man."

What history lies behind this tradition? One argument frequently heard today is that the gospels speak of the brothers and sisters of Jesus (Mark 6:3; Matt 13:55; Luke 8:19), and therefore he must have had siblings. The traditional argument is that the Greek *adelphos*, "brother," can also mean "cousin." John P. Meier offers a careful review of the question. He notes that Paul, Mark, John, the Jewish historian Josephus, and perhaps Luke in Acts 1:1 speak independently of the "brothers" of Jesus, that Josephus does distinguish between "brother" and "cousin," that the New Testament does not offer a single case where the *adelphos* means "cousin" or "stepbrother," and that Paul who had met "James the brother of the Lord" personally (Gal 1:19) was simply reflecting long tradition. He concludes that from a purely philological and historical point of view, the most probable opinion is that Jesus had siblings.[3]

There is however some internal evidence that could lead to a different conclusion. Both Mark 15:40 and Matthew 27:56 place at the crucifixion some women, Mary Magdalene, Salome, and "Mary the mother of the younger James and of Joses" (James and Joseph in Matthew). If James and Joses (or Joseph) are to be understood as the siblings of Jesus (Mark 6:3; Matt 13:55), it is very strange to identify Mary at the crucifixion by referring to her as their mother, rather than as the mother of Jesus. It is

---

[3] John P. Meier, *A Marginal Jew: Rethinking the Historical Jesus*, Vol I: *The Roots of the Problem and the Person* (New York: Doubleday, 1991) 331–32.

also true that even today "brother" in the Middle East is used as a form of address for male members of one's extended family. While it may be impossible to decide this question on biblical grounds, the teaching of the church is clear that Mary remained a virgin.

Mary in the Catholic Tradition

Mary has held an important place in the Catholic tradition since the earliest centuries of the church. Since other Christian traditions do not always share this Catholic devotion to Mary, we should consider how she came to occupy such an important place in Catholic life and faith. Catholic Mariology includes hymns and prayers, devotions like Marian novenas, May crownings, and the rosary, Marian statues, and apparitions. The church has many prayers addressed to Mary. The "Hail Holy Queen" (*Salve Regina*) dates from about the year 1000. Perhaps the most popular is the "Hail Mary." Though it developed even later, most of it is based on Scripture.

> Hail Mary,
> full of grace,
> the Lord is with thee.
> Blessed art thou among women,
> and Blessed is the fruit
> of thy womb, Jesus.
> Holy Mary,
> Mother of God
> pray for us sinners now
> and at the hour of our death,
> Amen.

The first verse is based on Luke 1:28, the second, Elizabeth's greeting to Mary, comes from Luke 1:42; they have been used together since the twelfth century. The concluding invocation of Mary as Mother of God and petition for help at the hour of death is from the fifteenth century. The prayer is also common in Orthodox Christianity, though with a slightly different final verse.

Much of Mariology falls into the category of popular religion; that is to say these devotions and traditions reflect popular expressions of Catholic faith and the devotion of Catholic people unique to a given culture; thus, they represent the inculturation of the faith in the symbols and iconography of a particular people.

For example, Our Lady of Guadalupe, the image of Mary so popular to Mexicans and Mexican Americans, is portrayed in the iconography of the indigenous people of Mexico. The apparition of the Virgin to the mestizo Juan Diego took place according to the tradition in 1531, ten years after the conquest of the Aztec capital of Tenochtitlan. The woman whose image appears on Juan Diego's mantel is brown-skinned, like the Indian people who still refer to her as "La Morenita," the little brown one. Some have argued that the image represents the Aztec goddess Tonantzin, the lunar mother goddess. But the fact that the Virgin stands on the moon and blocks the light of the sun, both worshipped by the indigenous peoples, is a way of asserting her superiority to the old religion, and thus the superiority of Christianity. In his study of Our Lady of Guadalupe, David Brading argues that whether the image was produced miraculously, as the story maintains, or by human artifice makes no difference: "as much as any icon, the Virgin of Tepeyac silently taught the truths of revelation as effectively as scripture since, like the gospels, the image was conceived through the inspiration of the Holy Spirit."[4] The church has generally made room in its devotional life for such popular expressions of Catholic faith, though its official teaching on Mary is much more limited. There are four Marian dogmas.

Perpetual Virginity

Although Scripture teaches only the virginal conception of Jesus, as we have seen, the belief in the perpetual virginity of Mary was first suggested by the apocryphal Protoevangelium of James (ca. 150). Athanasius (d. 373), Epiphanius (d. 404), and Jerome (d. 419) each attest to the idea. It was taught officially by the Second Council of Constantinople (553), which referred to Mary as "ever virgin."

Mother of God

About the same time that one finds these first references to the perpetual virginity of Mary, the title Mother of God (Greek: *theotokos*, literally "Godbearer"), begins to appear. It was used as early as 220 in the church's prayer. The title, christological in its reference, was confirmed by the First Council of Ephesus in 431.

The title *theotokos* shows how prayer and theology developed together in the early church. In the words of the famous church historian Jaroslav

---

[4] David A. Brading, *Mexican Phoenix: Our Lady of Guadalupe: Image and Tradition across Five Centuries* (Cambridge: Cambridge University Press, 2001) 366.

Pelikan, the sources for calling Mary *theotokos* "are almost certainly to be sought neither in polemics nor in speculation, but in devotion, perhaps in an early Greek version of the hymn to Mary, *'Sub Tuum Praesidium.'*[5] This beautiful prayer, used by both the Eastern and the Western Church, is very ancient: it can be traced back to a third-century Egyptian text.

> We fly to thy patronage,
> O holy Mother of God;
> Despise not our petitions
> in our necessities,
> but deliver us always from all dangers,
> O glorious and blessed Virgin,
> Amen.

Thus the practice of asking Mary's intercession is deeply rooted in the church's life.

The Immaculate Conception

The belief in the immaculate conception of Mary has long been held by the Eastern fathers. Augustine rejected it, reasoning that Mary as one born of conjugal intercourse shared in original sin, though she remained free from personal sin. Some theologians in the West followed Augustine's teaching. Others accepted the Eastern tradition. Pope Pius IX, stressing that Mary shared in the grace of salvation from the moment of her conception, formally defined the dogma in 1854. It is really a statement about God's special care for the mother of Jesus, preserving her from the taint of original sin, thus a statement about how dependent we are upon our own parents.

The Assumption

The dogma of the Assumption was celebrated liturgically in both the East and the West from the seventh century on, though some sources trace the feast to the fourth century. Pope Pius XII formally defined the dogma in 1950, teaching that "the Immaculate Mother of God, the ever Virgin Mary, having completed the course of her earthly life, was assumed body and soul into heavenly glory" (DS 3903). The dogma is really a statement that Mary shares fully in the resurrection of her Son.

---

[5] Jaroslav Pelikan, *The Emergence of the Catholic Tradition (100–600)* (Chicago: University of Chicago Press, 1971) 241.

When the resurrection takes place for all the just remains a mystery. Popular eschatology looks forward to the reunion of soul and body at the resurrection on the last day. But this remains at best an attempt to insert the spiritual or eschatological into a temporal framework in which it doesn't really fit. For example, it is unclear how a soul without the body would really be personal. Aquinas suggested that the separated soul is dependent on infused intelligible species and therefore knows only in a limited way. But his position is not without contradiction. According to Caroline Walker Bynum, "it is not finally clear whether Thomas places primary emphasis on soul as substantial form, united with God in beatific vision and spilling forth its glory in an expression of self we call body, or whether he gives first importance to the substance *homo*, whose component parts are each incomplete without the other."[6] Today some theologians argue that what the church has affirmed of Mary is true of all the just, that is, that they enter into glory at the moment of their death. In any case, the assumption of Mary prefigures her share in the resurrection of her son to which we all look forward in hope.

It is important to note that both Marian dogmas, the Immaculate Conception and the Assumption, were made only after the popes had consulted the faith of the church by a polling of the bishops.

Conclusion

Many years ago I had a heated dinner conversation with a Jesuit friend, a distinguished theologian, about the virgin birth. He said that he believed in it firmly, but "symbolically, not literally." I remember that I responded, "You can't pray the Creed with footnotes!"

The church does not consider the virgin birth of Jesus "just" a symbol. While it remains something we have to take on faith, we accept it as something the Christian tradition has taught since the beginning and which is now official doctrine. The church has a long tradition honoring Mary as "virgin" and "Mother of God," both of which are primarily statements about its belief in her son.

What *if* the virginal conception of Jesus *was* just a symbol? Would that affect our faith? Not so, according to no less an authority than Joseph Ratzinger, now Pope Benedict XVI, who says with remarkable lucidity:

---

[6] Caroline Walker Bynum, *The Resurrection of the Body in Western Christianity, 200–1336* (New York: Columbia University Press, 1995) 268–69.

. . . the doctrine of Jesus' divinity would not be affected if Jesus had been the product of a normal human marriage. For the Divine Sonship of which faith speaks is not a biological but an ontological fact, an event not in time but in God's eternity; God is always Father, Son, and Spirit; the conception of Jesus means, not that a new God-the-Son comes into being, but that God as Son in the man Jesus draws the creature man to himself, so that he himself "is" man.[7]

The doctrine of the virgin birth is one way of saying that the coming of the divine Word into space and time and human history is not just another purely human event; it is an act of God that came about by God's creative power through the Holy Spirit. At the same time, the Incarnation also required the cooperation of a young Jewish girl who in some mysterious way said yes: "May it be done to me according to your word" (Luke 1:38).

Mary has been considered as the "New Eve" and a type of the church from the early centuries of the church. Just as in Genesis 3:15 God says to the serpent: "I will put enmity between you and the woman, / and between your offspring and hers; / He will strike at your head, / while you strike at his heel," so Mary, virgin mother of the savior, has frequently been represented in Christian art as crushing the head of the ancient serpent.

In the Middle Ages a much more personal Marian cult developed and increasing emphasis was placed on her role in the work of redemption, which seemed to place her above the church. In spite of the fact that many of the Reformers shared to a considerable degree in the Marian piety of the ancient church, the Protestant reaction to what was seen as the excesses of Catholic Marian piety meant that devotion to Mary virtually disappeared from later Protestantism. Today there is a movement to reclaim a more biblical Marian piety within some segments of evangelical Christianity.[8]

---

[7] Joseph Ratzinger, *Introduction to Christianity* (San Francisco: Ignatius Press, 2004) 274–75.

[8] See Timothy George, "The Blessed Evangelical Mary: Why We Shouldn't Ignore Her Anymore," *Christianity Today* 47, no. 12 (December 2003) 34–39; also Tim Perry, *Mary for Evangelicals: Toward an Understanding of the Mother of the Lord* (Downers Grove, IL: InterVarsity, 2006).

Chapter 8

"He suffered under Pontius Pilate, was crucified, died, and was buried. He descended into hell."

We have seen how in the early centuries of Christianity the Docetists denied the humanity of Jesus, and thus, that the Son of God had truly died. Yet this is one of the great truths of Christianity. As Rabbi Harold Kushner writes with generous insight from a Jewish perspective, "Christianity introduced the world to the idea of a God who suffers, alongside the image of a God who creates and commands."[1]

The emphasis in the Apostles' Creed on Jesus' burial should be understood in terms of the Creed's original role in Christian baptism. In Paul's theology of baptism, the baptismal ritual in which the one being baptized was immersed in the baptismal water, literally being "buried" in the waters and then raised up again, symbolized the Christian's incorporation into the death and resurrection of Jesus: "We were indeed buried with him through baptism into death, so that, just as Christ was raised from the dead by the glory of the Father, we too might live in newness of life" (Rom 6:4; cf. Col 2:12). Thus Christian baptism incorporates one into Christ's Paschal mystery. For the new Christian it means dying to all that is not God and rising to new life in Christ.

---

[1] Harold S. Kushner, *When Bad Things Happen to Good People* (New York: Schocken Books, 1981) 85.

The Death of Jesus

But *why* did Jesus die? As a human being Jesus would have had to one day face death, as each of us must. But his death was a horrifying, humiliating experience, a judicial execution at the hands of imperial power. There had to be some particular historical reasons which occasioned it.

Among his criteria for recovering the history that lies behind the gospels, John Meier lists that of "Rejection and Execution." He reasons that there must have been something revolutionary about Jesus; "a bland Jesus who simply told people to look at the lilies of the field—such a Jesus would threaten no one."[2] Various reasons have been given for his death. Some believe that the Romans, seeing him as a revolutionary stirring up the people against the Roman occupation, took steps to do away with him. Others blame the Jewish religious authorities, especially representatives of the priesthood; they accuse them of conspiring with the Roman authorities because of his criticism of them, or for his reinterpretation of the Law, or for claiming to be God's Son.

The gospels suggest a combination of these reasons. Mark offers a number of charges against Jesus that surfaced at his trial, both religious and political: a threat to destroy the Temple (Mark 14:58), the charge of blasphemy, claiming to be "the Messiah, the son of the Blessed One" (Mark 14:61), and being a false prophet (Mark 14:65). At his trial before Pilate Jesus was accused of having messianic pretensions, which certainly would have been seen as a threat by the Romans (Mark 15:2).

Can modern scholarship discern behind the theology of the gospel accounts the offense that led to the death of Jesus? Today a number of scholars think that the clue to Jesus' offense can be glimpsed in an action of Jesus reflected in the story of his cleansing the Temple (Mark 11:15-16; Matt 21:12-13; Luke 19:45-46; and John 2:13-20).[3] More than righteous anger at what seemed to be a desecration of his Father's house, turning it into "a den of thieves" (Mark 11:17; cf. Jer 7:11), Jesus' Temple action was more likely a symbol that the time for the Temple and its cult was at an end. In doing so, he was striking at the heart of official Jewish religious life.

---

[2] John P. Meier, *A Marginal Jew: Rethinking the Historical Jesus*, Vol I: *The Roots of the Problem and the Person* (New York: Doubleday, 1991) 177.

[3] N. T. Wright, *Jesus and the Victory of God* (Minneapolis, MN: Fortress, 1996) 405; cf. 370; see also Walter Kasper, *Jesus the Christ* (New York: Paulist, 1977) 117; Raymond E. Brown, *The Death of the Messiah*, Vol. I (New York: Doubleday, 1994) 460.

The movement that Jesus began during his ministry, gathering disciples, placing the Twelve at their center, proclaiming that the reign of God was at hand, symbolized a renewed or eschatological Israel. But his movement understandably generated considerable opposition from the religious leaders of Israel, particularly from the high priests whose power depended on their cooperation with the occupying Roman power. They did not welcome his message. Jesus' journey to Jerusalem in the final days of his ministry would have brought him and his movement into conflict with these authorities. This makes his action in the Temple all the more significant. In driving out the money changers and those who sold the animals for sacrifice, he was effectively shutting down, at least temporarily, the Temple's cult, marking the end of the old dispensation and the beginning of a new one. The charge that he claimed that he would destroy the Temple, which seems to have played an important role at his trial, may reflect a garbled retelling of the Temple incident in the gospels. Joseph Ratzinger is among those who accept this view. In a book on the liturgy, he argues that with the Resurrection, the body of Christ made present in the Eucharist in his self-offering or sacrifice to the Father becomes the new Temple, the true place of meeting between God and God's people. The story in the Synoptic Gospels of the tearing of the veil of the Temple, from top to bottom, symbolizes that the time of the old Temple has come to an end.[4]

Some commentators, particularly those in the controversial Jesus Seminar, seek to deny any Jewish involvement in Jesus' condemnation, dismissing the narrative of Mark's gospel, including its passion account, as pure theology or theological creativity.[5] But we are not dependent solely on the gospels for the story of Jesus' death. Paul acknowledges Jewish involvement (1 Thess 2:14-15). So does the Jewish historian Josephus. His *Jewish Antiquities* (ca. 93), once purged of what seem to be later Christian interpolations, provides another source for the story of Jesus, no matter how brief:

> At this time there appeared Jesus, a wise man. For he was a doer of startling deeds, a teacher of people who receive the truth with pleasure. And he gained a following both among many Jews and among many of Greek

[4] Joseph Ratzinger, *The Spirit of the Liturgy* (San Francisco: Ignatius Press, 2000) 43.

[5] Cf. John Dominic Crossan, *The Historical Jesus: The Life of a Mediterranean Jewish Peasant* (HarperSanFrancisco, 1991) 389–90; Burton L. Mack, *A Myth of Innocence: Mark and Christian Origins* (Philadelphia: Fortress Press, 1988) 371.

origin. And when Pilate, because of an accusation made by the leading men among us, condemned him to the cross, those who had loved him previously did not cease to do so. And up until this very day the tribe of Christians (named after him) has not died out.[6]

The Creed mentions that Jesus was crucified under Pontius Pilate, the Roman governor at the time. Like so many in history, Jesus was the victim of the abuse of military and political power. If some of the Jewish leaders conspired with the Roman authorities to condemn him, this does not mean that the Jewish people collectively were guilty of his death. Unfortunately, this has frequently been alleged over the centuries, from Melito of Sardis in the early second century to a never published draft of an encyclical on racism and Nazi ideology, prepared for Pope Pius XI in 1938.[7]

The result has been a long and tragic history of anti-Semitism, with charges of "deicide," persecutions, pogroms, and slanders such as the myth of the ritual murder of Christian children by Jews, culminating in the Holocaust during the Second World War.[8] The Second Vatican Council addressed this specifically; it taught that the Jews "remain most dear to God," rejecting the notion of collective Jewish guilt, either on the part of those living at the time of Jesus or today (NA 4).

The Descent into Hell

To the phrase "was crucified, died, and was buried," the Apostles' Creed adds "He descended into hell" (*ad inferna*). This strange expression, first appearing in the Creed in the mid-fourth century, affirms that Jesus truly died, that he "went down" to the realm of the dead (Hebrew: *Sheol*, Greek: *Hades*), not to hell as the state of the damned.[9] In Hebrew thought, to say that someone went down to Sheol meant simply that the person had died. Of course this language of descent, like that of ascent,

---

[6] Cited by Meier, *A Marginal Jew*, 61.

[7] See Philip A. Cunningham, "Uncharted Waters: The Future of Catholic-Jewish Relations," 133, no. 13 *Commonweal* (July 14, 2006) 11–12.

[8] See Edward H. Flannery, *The Anguish of the Jews: Twenty-Three Centuries of Anti-Semitism* (New York: Paulist Press, 1985).

[9] The phrase "descended into hell" is sometimes translated "descended to the dead." This translation avoids confusion about the descent into hell by stressing that Jesus truly died.

is metaphorical. The Word is always in the bosom of the Father, at the Father's right hand. But the man Jesus to whom the Word was united truly died; just as he entered fully into human life, so also he shared completely in the finality of death. In another sense, given the terrible circumstances of his crucifixion, we can say that in his Passion Jesus descended into the hell of abandonment and isolation.

Still, the phrase "descended into hell" remains a challenge to interpreters. In the earliest tradition, reflected in writers such as Ignatius of Antioch, Polycarp, Irenaeus, and Tertullian, the descent meant simply that Jesus had truly died and gone down to the realm of the dead.[10] Some understood the descent in light of 1 Peter 3:19-20, which speaks of Christ going after his death "to preach to the spirits in prison," in other words, to bring about the conversion of those living in the netherworld. From the context here, those spirits have been seen as the souls of the righteous who died before the redemption and now share in Christ's victory (cf. 1 Pet 4:6). In the East there was often a soteriological dimension to the descent; Christ opens the gates of Sheol, bringing the righteous the good news of his victory over death. This was powerfully expressed in an ancient sermon for Holy Saturday, now part of *The Liturgy of the Hours*:

> Something strange is happening—there is a great silence on earth today, a great silence and stillness. The whole earth keeps silence because the King is asleep. The earth trembled and is still because God has fallen asleep in the flesh and he has raised up all who have slept ever since the world began. God has died in the flesh and hell trembles with fear.
>
> He has gone to search for our first parent, as for a lost sheep. Greatly desiring to visit those who live in darkness and in the shadow of death, he has gone to free from sorrow the captives Adam and Eve. The Lord approached them bearing the cross, the weapon that had won him the victory. At the sight of him Adam, the first man he had created, struck his breast and cried out to everyone, "My Lord be with you all." Christ answered him: "And with your spirit." He took him by the hand and raised him up, saying: Awake, O sleeper, and rise from the dead, and Christ will give you light.[11]

---

[10] "The frequent New Testament affirmations that Jesus was 'raised from the dead' presuppose that the crucified one sojourned in the realm of the dead prior to his resurrection"; *Catechism of the Catholic Church*, no. 632.

[11] From an ancient homily on Holy Saturday, PG 43, 439, 451, 462–63.

The soteriological sense of Christ's victory over death and Satan spread also to the West. This story—"the harrowing of hell"—the Old English term for the descent, has long been celebrated in English literature.

Two modern commentators give the story of the descent a more existential interpretation, stressing the radical abandonment of Jesus in his death. Hans Urs von Balthasar places the descent at the center of his christology. Meditating on this mystery from a more subjective perspective, he sees in it a description of Christ's entering fully into the forsakenness of the dead, completely alone, cut off even from God. Just as Jesus during his life had been in solidarity with all the living, so also in his death he entered into solidarity with the dead, with all the children of Adam who must face this ultimate fate. But precisely by entering into that darkness as the Son of God, he makes it possible for others to find God there, even in death, perhaps even in hell.[12] Von Balthasar's interpretation, with its hint of universal salvation, remains controversial.

Joseph Ratzinger sees in the "descent into hell" a symbol of the modern experience of the absence or "death" of God, but also a sign of hope in the midst of hopelessness. The phrase reminds us not just of God's speech, but also of God's silence, again the great mystery of Holy Saturday recalled in the liturgy. Jesus' cry of utter abandonment on the cross, "My God, my God, why have you forsaken me?" (Mark 15:34) becomes the cry of modern men and women who experience themselves as fearful, abandoned, in that state of absolute loneliness theology calls "hell." What the article on the descent into hell asserts is "that Christ strode through the gate of our final loneliness, that in his Passion he went down into the abyss of our abandonment. Where no voice can reach us any longer, there is he." If the "second death" (Rev 20:14) remains a possibility, what Ratzinger calls our "deliberate self-enclosure in hell" or our deliberate rejection of God, for the just hell and death are no longer. "The door of death stands open since life—love—has dwelt in death."[13]

Theological Perspectives

The earliest Christians, though shocked by the death of Jesus, were convinced from the beginning that he was with them in a new way. As

---

[12] See Hans Urs von Balthasar, "Going to the Dead: Holy Saturday," in his *Mysterium Paschale* (Edinburgh: T & T Clark, 1990) 148–188, esp. 174–79.

[13] Joseph Ratzinger, *Introduction to Christianity* (San Francisco: Ignatius Press, 2004) 293–301 at 301.

they struggled to find meaning in his death, they drew on Old Testament motifs, the rejected prophet (1 Thess 2:15-16; Luke 11:49-51; Acts 7:51-53), the suffering righteous one (Luke 24:25, 44-46; Matt 27:39-43; cf. Wis 2:10-22), and increasingly on the idea of a redemptive death (1 Cor 15:3b-5; Gal 1:4; Rom 4:25; 5:8; Eph 5:2; Mark 10:45). A very early creed, cited by Paul, says that Christ died for our sins (1 Cor 15:3; cf. Rom 5:8; 2 Cor 5:21; Gal 3:13). Mark reports Jesus as saying, "the Son of Man did not come to be served but to serve and to give his life as a ransom for many" (Mark 10:45). In the eucharistic words of institution Jesus says, "This is my body, which will be given for you . . . This cup is the new covenant in my blood, which will be shed for you" (Luke 22:19-20).

The idea that Christ's death itself was salvific could not have entered the tradition so early if it was not in some way rooted in what Jesus himself did and said in his ministry. As Edward Schillebeeckx has written:

> Jesus felt his death to be (in some way or other) part and parcel of the salvation—offered—by—God, as a historical consequence of his caring and loving service of and solidarity with people. This is the very least—albeit certain—thing about the 'institution narrative' and the account of the Passion that we are bound to hang on to as a historical core.[14]

From the beginning, the saving significance of Jesus' death was celebrated liturgically. In writing to the church of Corinth in the mid 50s, Paul reminds them, "as often as you eat this bread and drink the cup, you proclaim the death of the Lord until he comes" (1 Cor 11:26). Memorial (*anamnesis*), proclamation (*kerygma*), thanksgiving (*eucharistia*), and discerning the body are at the center of the Eucharist. It is the celebration of the new covenant in Christ's blood (1 Cor 11:25; Luke 22:20).

Paul uses a rich variety of metaphors to express what God had done for us in Christ.[15] The most common is the word justification, meaning that because of Christ we are forgiven our sins, thus enabled to stand before God as righteous. Also common is the word salvation, in the sense of our being rescued from evil, but with a clear future reference as well. Paul develops this with his typology of Adam, the first man, bringing sin

---

[14] Edward Schillebeeckx, *Jesus: An Experiment in Christology* (New York: Seabury, 1979) 310.

[15] See Joseph A. Fitzmyer, "Pauline Theology," in *The New Jerome Biblical Commentary*, ed. Raymond E. Brown, Joseph A. Fitzmyer, and Roland E. Murphy (Englewood Cliffs, NJ: Prentice Hall, 1990) 1397–1401.

and death, while Christ, the second man or last Adam breaks the power of death, bringing life, both now and in the world to come (Rom 5; 1 Cor 15:45-49). Other metaphors include reconciliation, expiation, redemption, freedom, sanctification, transformation, new creation, and glorification.

The Fourth Gospel tells the story of Jesus as the Word of God breaking into our world as light and life. The cross, the lifting up of Jesus, is also his glorification (John 13:31-32), his gathering into one God's people (John 11:49-52), drawing all to himself (John 12:32), revealing his unity with the Father (John 8:28), and offering life to those who believe in his name (John 20:31). The language here is different from the language of sacrifice so strong in Paul.

The Eastern fathers, strongly influenced by the Johannine tradition, emphasized the anthropological consequences of the Incarnation. More mystical and speculative, they see creation itself as elevated and humanity transformed, even divinized (*theōsis, theopoesis*), as a result of the Word becoming flesh. Cyril of Alexandria (d. 444), more cautious about using the vocabulary of divinization, prefers to speak of our share in the divine life, but by grace, not by nature (cf. 2 Pet 1:4).[16] Other themes expressive of the new life or salvation in Christ, prominent in the fathers of the church but with roots in the New Testament, include victory, atonement, revelation, eschatological judgment, and exemplar.[17]

In contrast to the mystical theology of the East, the more practical Western fathers, raised in a culture dominated by law and commerce, tended to place more emphasis on redemption and the idea of satisfaction, "on a transaction performed in Jesus" to free us from our sins.[18] Tertullian, using economic terms, speaks of Jesus' death as "earnest-money on the principle."[19] The idea of Jesus as "ransom" paid to the devil to free us from our sins seems strange to us, but it occurs in Irenaeus (d. 200), Origen (d. ca. 254), Gregory of Nyssa (335–94), Rufinus (d. 411), and Augustine (354–430); Jesus is bait, like a fish on a hook (Gregory) or a mouse in a trap (Augustine).

Augustine presents Christ's work as both ransom and sacrifice. In Book 13 of his great book *De Trinitate*, Christ's death is the ransom paid

---

[16] See Daniel A. Keating, *The Appropriation of Divine Life in Cyril of Alexandria* (Oxford: Oxford University Press, 2004) 10–11.

[17] Michael Slusser, "Primitive Christian Soteriological Themes," *Theological Studies* 44 (1983) 555–69.

[18] Thus Roger Haight, *Jesus Symbol of God* (Maryknoll, NY: Orbis, 1999) 223.

[19] Tertullian, *De Resurr. Mort* 51/1–3; cf. *Adv. Marc.* III 9/4.

to Satan, into whose power humankind had fallen, not because of God who is just, but because of the sin of our first parents which had alienated them from God.[20] Augustine also describes Christ as the innocent victim offered to God as a "propitiation" which makes satisfaction for the sins of humankind (*Trin.* 4.13.17). From this comes the theory of substitution; Christ died in our place for our sins.

It was Anselm of Canterbury's (d. 1109) powerful rereading of Augustine that was to indelibly stamp Western theology, particularly evangelical theology, down to our own time. In his *Cur Deus Homo?* (*Why God Became Man*), he explains the Incarnation as the divine response to Adam's sin. Since the sin was against an infinite being, it was an infinite offense, breaking the order of creation. Forgiveness would not restore that order, punishment would have to be eternal, and so only satisfaction by an infinite being could make the infinite satisfaction owed for such an offense. Behind Anselm's reasoning here is the highly developed feudal sense of the honor owed the nobility and the satisfaction due such a person for an offense. Furthermore, to respect both the established order of creation and human freedom, humanity must be somehow involved. The result is the Incarnation.

Luther combined Anselm's theology of satisfaction with Augustine's concept of substitution; Jesus takes our place, pays our penalty, becoming himself the satisfaction for our sins. In the later Reformation tradition this became known as the doctrine of "penal satisfaction." While simple and clear, it has the unhappy consequence of reducing the various metaphors for God's salvific work in Christ, and thus the Incarnation itself, to one, making satisfaction for sins. God became human because humans had sinned. Gone is the sense, so strong in Eastern theology, of the transformation of the human (*theōsis*, divinization) because of the Incarnation, or the sense that it is the entire mystery of Jesus—life, death, and resurrection, which is salvific—not just his death. This practical neglect of the life of Jesus narrows the Gospel down to an individualistic doctrine of salvation. Consequently, little attention is given to Jesus' proclamation of the reign of God, his identification with the poor and suffering, or his call to discipleship. In much of Protestant evangelical theology, all one has to do is to be "born again." If one has been "saved," he or she can be certain of salvation. From this perspective even membership in the church becomes less important.

[20] See Haight, *Jesus Symbol of God*, 224–26.

Satisfaction theology also detracts from the image of God as a loving Father, suggesting that God required the death of his only begotten Son as the price of our salvation, a view that still holds pride of place among evangelicals.[21] And there are theological problems with this approach. Explaining salvation in terms of satisfaction theology introduces the problematic concept of a transaction that restores humanity to communion with God, as well as "the metaphysically impossible idea of a transformation of God."[22] Pastorally, it has led to an emphasis on God's wrath in Christian preaching and spirituality, obscuring the gratuitous love of God. Ratzinger argues that the "divine-*cum*-human-legal system erected by Anselm" can "make the image of God appear in a sinister light."[23]

Though never formally defined by the church, Anselm's theory of satisfaction has achieved quasi-magisterial authority in evangelical theology. It is often present in popular Catholicism and appears again in the *Catechism of the Catholic Church* (no. 615). But it is only one way of conceiving of God's grace offered us in the life, death, and resurrection of Jesus, a second order theological language removed by several levels of metaphor and interpretation from the experiences of the first disciples.

Abelard (d. 1142) provided an alternative to Anselm's view; he saw the Incarnation as an act of love that was both revelational and exemplary, showing us how to love both God and our neighbor. Others have followed Abelard's lead; they see salvation in Christ as embodying the mystery of God with us and gathering us into a share in the divine life. Liberation theology, without denying the resurrection of the body, focuses on salvation in the biblical sense of God's bringing justice to the poor and oppressed. The cross as a symbol of our salvation, teaches us that we must renounce hatred and violence, placing ourselves completely in the hands of God, just as Jesus did. The cross and the resurrection of Jesus reveal that God's love is stronger than death. All of these metaphors and theologies are important for understanding God's offer of new life in Christ which enables us to share in God's life and makes us

---

[21] See Mark Dever, "Nothing But the Blood," *Christianity Today* 50, no. 5 (May 2006) 28–33.

[22] Karl Rahner, "The Universality of Salvation," in *Theological Investigations* 16 (New York: Seabury, 1979) 208.

[23] Joseph Ratzinger, *Introduction to Christianity* (San Francisco: Ignatius Press, 2004) 233.

part of a new people.[24] Thus Jesus mediates an experience of God that is truly life-changing.

Conclusion

I don't regularly visit cemeteries. And yet it is always a powerful experience for me to do so. They are peaceful places, quiet, often beautiful. Being in the presence of the dead brings about a sense of reverence. Military cemeteries are particularly moving to visit. To see monuments for those who have lived full lives is not particularly painful; it brings a sense of fulfillment and closure. But military cemeteries, with crosses or stones in ranks and columns, speak of lives cut short, horrible sufferings, dreams unrealized, and the crushing finality of death.

I remember wandering the great military cemetery at Colleville Sur Mer overlooking Omaha Beach, where so many Americans who died in the 1944 invasion of Normandy are buried. Or the Punchbowl National Cemetery above Honolulu, where more than twenty-five thousand who died in the Pacific now rest. Once in Berlin, I noticed from my window a cemetery next door to the hotel where I was staying. I went out in the cold and drifting snow of a February morning to look at the stones, many of them simple military markers in straight lines. Most said simply "unknown," or "unknown soldier," silent testimony to the thousands who fell in battle or died in the terrible bombing raids on Berlin. In such places one can only reflect and pray.

And Jesus has been there. To confess that he suffered, died, and was buried is to remind ourselves how fully God has embraced our humanity, including our death. Today the humanity of Jesus is not a question for us; we take it for granted. But it has always fascinated me that for many exposed to Christian teaching in the early days of the church, what was difficult to accept was not the divinity of Jesus, but precisely his humanity. Jesus truly suffered agony, torture, and death. He descended into hell. We should not spiritualize his death. As God wept for the sufferings of his only beloved Son, so God weeps with us in our sufferings and is in solidarity with us in our pain.

If Christ's victory is also ours, it does not mean that we will not suffer ourselves in what we recognize in our prayer as "this vale of tears."

---

[24] See Thomas P. Rausch, "A Contemporary Approach to Soteriology," in *Who Is Jesus? An Introduction to Christology* (Collegeville, MN: Liturgical Press, 2003) 183–202.

Suffering is unavoidable, especially for those who seek to follow Jesus. The church has sometimes attempted to consecrate suffering with a false mysticism, counseling patience and forbearance for the poor and the marginal, assuring them of comfort hereafter. That is why Karl Marx referred to Christianity as an opiate for the poor.

But it is equally an abuse of the Christian tradition to suggest that suffering can be eliminated through earthly utopias, egalitarian societies, or even a democratic church. This is not to justify oppressive structures, but to recall what Jesus taught, that each of us must take up the cross (Mark 8:34) or that the seed must die if it is to bear fruit (John 12:24). In haunting words Paul reminds us that our own sufferings fill up what is lacking in the suffering of Christ on behalf of his body, the church (Col 1:24).

The church's doctrine of salvation grew out of the disciples' Easter experience of their new life in Christ. As they struggled to find meaning in the scandal of his brutal execution, they drew on the metaphors and images of their religious culture. In the West, Anselm's theory of satisfaction, also culturally inspired, gained quasi-dogmatic status. Certainly other theological metaphors such as atonement, reconciliation, redemption, justification, satisfaction, recapitulation, or divinization can help us to better understand what God has done in Christ, though we need to avoid literalizing any one of them.

It is true that the New Testament uses the language of sacrifice. Paul does. The letter to the Hebrews presents Jesus as both high priest and sacrifice (Heb 7). A sacrifice, however, is not necessarily bloody, but a symbolic self-offering which brings about greater communion between God and God's people. Joseph Ratzinger notes that while sacrifice is at the heart of worship in most religions, the notion of sacrifice has been buried under endless misunderstandings. Sacrifice does not necessarily have anything to do with destruction, but with moving from a state of separation or autonomy to one of surrender to God.[25] The theme is constant in the Old Testament:

> For you do not desire sacrifice;
>> A burnt offering you would not accept.
> My sacrifice is a broken spirit;
>> God, do not spurn a broken, humbled heart.
>> (Ps 51:18-19)[26]

---

[25] Ratzinger, *The Spirit of the Liturgy*, 27–28.
[26] See also 1 Sam 15:22; Hos 6:6; Ps 50:12-14; Matt 9:13; 12:7.

Jesus' sacrifice was not a bloody payment to satisfy the injured dignity of God or to make amends for an infinite offense against God's justice, but the total self-offering of a beloved Son, whose union with his Father was total, in his living as well as in his dying. God does not ask satisfaction, God welcomes and embraces the wayward child, as Jesus taught us in his parable of the Prodigal Son (Luke 15:11-32).

If justification, redemption, and atonement are central metaphors for God's salvific work in Christ, other traditions have remained faithful to the experience of the early Christians by using the language of healing, transformation, victory over sin and death, and revelation. Jesus himself is the way, the truth, and the life. He was the just one; he did not respond to evil with evil, to violence with violence. In showing us the way to the Father he does not ask us to go where he has not first gone himself. We can find him even there.

Chapter 9

"On the third day he rose again. He ascended into heaven and is seated at the right hand of the Father. He will come again to judge the living and the dead."

The New Testament tradition begins with the news that Jesus, the crucified one, has been raised up. The message is clear; one finds it everywhere in the New Testament documents, and the story of Jesus' life in the gospels concludes with accounts of his resurrection and appearances to his own. The resurrection of Jesus is clearly seen by the New Testament authors, not just as God's vindication of Jesus, but also as our own promise of eternal life. We will consider the resurrection of the body in another chapter. In this chapter we will consider the resurrection of Jesus, his ascension, enthronement, and second coming.

The Resurrection

The New Testament expresses Jesus' personal victory over death in different ways. Some very early passages from the Q community, which seems to lack explicit proclamation of the Resurrection, look forward to Jesus coming again (*parousia*) as eschatological judge and savior (Luke 12:8-9; Matt 10:32-33); in other words Jesus, the crucified one, lives. Luke sometimes speaks of Jesus simply as being "alive" or "living" (Luke 24:5, 23). The expression "taken up in glory" is used in 1 Tim 3:16. The terms "exalted" or "exaltation" (*hypsō*) are used to express the idea that Jesus has been brought from the realm of the dead and enthroned "at the right hand of God" (Acts 2:33; cf. Phil 2:8-9). In John "exaltation" has a similar sense; it means being raised up on the cross, raised up from death, and raised up to the Father's presence (John 3:14; 8:28; 12:32). Resurrection, ascension, and glorification are one moment.

Christ's victory over death is most often expressed by the language of resurrection, by the Greek verb *egeirō*, meaning "to awaken" or "to raise up," as in "he was raised up" (Rom 4:25; 6:4; 7:4; 1 Cor 6:14; 15:4; Mark 16:6), or by the less frequent *anistēmi*, "to set erect," or "to make stand up" (Acts 2:24; Mark 9:9, 10, 31). In some places, exaltation is combined with resurrection as its consequence (Rom 1:4; Acts 2:32-33; 5:30-31; 1 Pet 1:2). Generally, being raised up is something that happens to Jesus, though occasionally the verb is in the active voice, as in Jesus "rose" from the dead (1 Thess 4:14; John 20:9), which is also the language of the Creed.

Two distinct strands of resurrection tradition can be discerned, the Easter proclamation or *kerygma*, and the Easter stories. The Easter kerygma, the earlier tradition, consists of short, formulaic, often liturgical proclamations that Jesus has been raised up. The kerygma is reportorial, not imaginative. Perhaps the oldest is one Paul himself was familiar with from his own catechesis:

> For I handed on to you as of first importance what I also received: that Christ died for our sins in accordance with the scriptures; that he was buried; that he was raised on the third day in accordance with the scriptures. (1 Cor 15:3-5)

Other examples would include: "The gospel about his Son, descended from David according to the flesh, but established as Son of God in power according to the spirit of holiness through resurrection from the dead" (Rom 1:3-4), or the creedal "if you confess with your mouth that Jesus is Lord and believe in your heart that God raised him from the dead, you will be saved" (Rom 10:9).

The Easter stories developed later. There are two types, stories of the discovery of the empty tomb and imaginative accounts of the appearances of the risen Jesus to the disciples. Mark's gospel, the earliest, originally concluded without an appearance story, though it includes a story of the discovery of the empty tomb, along with the proclamation that Jesus has been raised up and would precede the disciples to Galilee (Mark 16:1-8). The so-called "longer ending" of Mark (16:9-20) summarizes some of the appearance stories from the gospels of Matthew and Luke; it was obviously composed later.

The Easter stories are not literal accounts of the disciples' "Easter experience"; they are in large part theological stories reflective of the Easter faith of the first disciples and the early Christian communities, written in order to help others come to that same faith. Thus we learn that the (Jewish) Scriptures teach us about Jesus (Luke 24:27, 44), that he remains with the community of the disciples always (Matt 28:18-20), that we encounter him in "the breaking of the bread" or Eucharist (Luke 24:31, 35; cf. John 20:21-23; Acts 10:41-42), in the forgiveness of sins (John 20:23), and that one does not have to see Jesus personally to be a believer (John 20:29). The risen Jesus is no longer limited by space and time; he appears when he wants and where he wants. Yet his risen body still bears the wounds of his Passion (John 20:27), suggesting that he is still in solidarity with us in our own brokenness, we who still live in this "vale of tears."

The Easter Experience

Thus the Easter stories in the gospels witness to the Easter faith of the earliest disciples. Just what their "Easter experience" actually was is difficult to assess. Paul, the only New Testament author who writes autobiographically, says simply, that God "was pleased to reveal (*apocalypsai*) his Son to me" (Gal 1:12, 16), though he also says in 1 Corinthians 9:1, "Have I not seen Jesus our Lord?" The later and much more dramatic story of his conversion, told three times in the Acts of the Apostles (Acts 9:1-9; 22:3-16; 26:2-8), really represents another Easter story. We do not know just *how* the risen Jesus manifested himself to the disciples. Did they actually see him? Was it some kind of interior illumination? Was it "a gracious gift of conversion to Jesus *as* the Christ" through Jesus himself, who discloses himself as the risen Christ in and through the grace of conversion, as Edward Schillebeeckx suggests?[1] We do not really know just *how* the disciples came to know and experience him after the crucifixion.

The Easter stories suggest that they came to faith gradually, as we must. Even given the report of the empty tomb, the disciples at first were frightened (Mark 16:8; Luke 24:37), unsure, did not recognize him

---

[1] Edward Schillebeeckx, *Jesus: An Experiment in Christology* (New York: Seabury Press, 1979) 384.

(Luke 24:16), thought that they were seeing a ghost (Luke 24:37); some remained incredulous, continuing to doubt (Matt 28:17). Even Mary Magdalene, who loved Jesus, did not recognize him, mistaking him for the gardener (John 20:14-15). The stories in Luke suggest that Jesus had to lead the disciples to Easter faith, explaining the Scriptures to them (Luke 24:32), breaking the bread in their presence (Luke 24:30), inviting them to touch him, and asking for something to eat (Luke 24:39-42).

However we understand the experiences of the disciples, these incidents "were not in their innermost essence . . . open to neutral observance or verification, but revelatory events in which the eschatological and christological significance of Jesus was disclosed."[2] If not a purely subjective experience, a sudden realization of the true significance of Jesus, as some theologians would suggest, neither was it an objective event, able to be perceived by any non-biased observer, a point made by Gerald O'Collins who also stresses the visual component in the appearances.[3] The risen Jesus did not manifest himself to the world. He did not return to Pilate, or to the high priest or to the Sanhedrin who handed him over (Mark 15:1), as we would like to have heard. Those whose hearts were closed to him could not experience the risen Jesus, for God then and now respects our freedom. Jesus appeared to his own, to those who had opened their hearts to him, who had followed him and loved him. Dermot Lane speaks of their experience as transformative; "Those who had followed Jesus in faith now come to recognize him in a different way as risen in light of their transforming experience of his new, real, personal presence."[4]

The resurrection of Jesus was a transcendent act of God on Jesus in his humanity, the divine vindication of his ministry. It might be properly categorized as an *eschatological* event, real but transcendent, touching history but beyond it. Jesus who went down to the abode of the dead, who truly died, has been raised up. To speak of the "bodily" resurrection of Jesus means that Jesus lives now with God, in his full humanity or personhood. He lives now in God's future, on the other side of space and time and human history. Thus the resurrection of Jesus cannot be proved, in the sense of a historical demonstration. It is not proved by

---

[2] Reginald H. Fuller, *The Foundations of the Resurrection Narratives* (New York: Macmillan, 1971) 48.

[3] Gerald O'Collins, *Christology: A Biblical, Historical, and Systematic Study of Jesus* (Oxford: Oxford University Press, 1995) 93.

[4] Dermot A. Lane, *The Reality of Jesus* (New York: Paulist Press, 1975) 61.

the empty tomb, though Matthew's story of the guards at the tomb is suggestive (Matt 28:11-15). There could not have been "film at eleven." All we can do is to point to what historically are the results of this act of God on Jesus, "the appearances, the empty tomb and the reality of Christianity itself."[5]

What is clear is that the disciples were absolutely convinced by their Easter experience, and changed by it. These frightened, timorous men who had abandoned Jesus in his Passion were transformed by their encounter with the risen Jesus. He did not rebuke them for abandoning him; rather Jesus greets them with a benediction, "peace" (Luke 24:36; John 20:21, 26), not merely assuring them of his continuing love, but sending them forth to preach (Gal 1:8; Mark 16:15; Luke 24:47), to teach and baptize (Matt 28:19-20), and to forgive sins (John 20:23). Peter, who betrayed him, is made pastor of the flock, the church (John 21:15-17). Jesus appeared also to some of the women in their group, most notably Mary Magdalene, who seems to have been the first to whom Jesus appeared, sending her to proclaim his resurrection to the other disciples (John 20:17; cf. Matt 28:10). In the early third century she was already called by Hippolytus the "apostle of the apostles." The memory of women among the New Testament witnesses suggests that they must have played an important role in early days of the church.

The Easter stories make clear that the encounter with the risen Jesus involved a mission; these men and women began to preach publicly, bringing the good news of the risen Christ's presence with his own to all who would listen. They began a movement which, within little more than fifty years, had turned what began as a sect within Judaism into a world religion.

The Ascension and Enthronement

The church's liturgical time celebrates Christ's ascension or return to the Father forty days after Easter, following Luke's story in the Acts of the Apostles (Acts 1:3), really another Easter story. In contrast to the Acts, in his gospel the Ascension takes place on Easter Sunday evening (Luke 24:51). But Luke's approach is idiosyncratic; most of the New Testament authors do not separate the resurrection and exaltation of Jesus, as we saw earlier. Thus the strange words of the risen Jesus to Mary

[5] Ibid., 45.

Magdalene in John: "Stop holding on to me, for I have not yet ascended to the Father" (John 20:17). The resurrection, ascension, and exaltation of Jesus are one event, as we have seen.

The Ascension is one way of symbolizing Jesus' return to the presence of God, though there are many others which proclaim that Jesus is now with God. The most common is the idea of his enthronement or exaltation "at the right hand" of God (Mark 14:62; 16:19; Luke 22:69; Acts 2:33-34; 7:55-56; Rom 8:34; Eph 1:20; Col 3:1; Heb 1:3; 8:1; 10:12; 1 Pet 3:22). John, with his very high christology, speaks frequently of Jesus "going" or "ascending" (John 13:1; 14:3; 16:5) or of his glorification (John 12:23; 16:14; 17:24).

Thus the gospels do not treat separately resurrection, ascension, and Pentecost, though we distinguish these mysteries in our liturgical celebrations. The Resurrection proclaims Jesus' victory over death; the Ascension symbolizes his return to the Father; his enthronement means that Jesus now exercises divine power and will come again.

The Second Coming

Because the resurrection of Jesus was experienced against the apocalyptic expectation of a general resurrection of the dead at the end of time (Dan 12:1-3), many Jewish Christians concluded that the end times had arrived. Interpreting his resurrection against this apocalyptic background, many of the early Christians looked forward to the imminent return of Jesus Christ as Lord (1 Cor 7:29; 1 Thess 4:15-16; Mark 9:1).

The idea of the Second Coming of Christ (Catholics often refer to it as the *parousia*, which means "presence," or "coming") has long been part of the Christian tradition. The early Christians looked forward to Christ's return with joy and expectation, crying out in their liturgy, "O Lord, come" (*marana tha*; 1 Cor 16:22; cf. Rev 22:20). Christ is our intercessor, one who shares our humanity; they looked forward to his coming in glory to bring us the fullness of salvation. The early Christians celebrated the Eucharist facing East, towards the rising sun, representing Christ who will come again.[6] But as Christians in the Middle Ages began to focus increasingly on the divinity of Jesus, his suffering for our sins, and his role as judge, the second coming became something dreaded and feared.

---

[6] Joseph Ratzinger, *The Spirit of the Liturgy* (San Francisco: Ignatius Press, 2000) 68, 82–83.

Crucifixes now prominent over the altars of churches vividly portrayed his sufferings. In the twelfth and thirteenth centuries many churches had representations of the general resurrection and final judgment in bas-relief sculptures over their doorways. The *Dies Irae*, a medieval sequence for the Requiem Mass dating from the thirteenth century, proclaimed that on that "day of wrath . . . even the just are mercy needing." The figure of the triumphant Christ coming to his own had been transformed into an image of a stern figure coming in judgment.

How should we understand the Creed's affirmation that Christ will come again to judge the living and the dead? Clearly how or when Christ will come again remains a mystery, yet the Second Coming remains a source of endless controversy. Jesus himself said that only the Father knows the day and the hour (Matt 24:36), and the New Testament is vague as to how our salvation will be fully realized. While it teaches that each of us must one day give an account of ourselves, it remains less clear on just how that will come about. Paul insists that all of us must one day stand before the judgment seat of God (Rom 14:10); he also sees Christ Jesus as sharing in this divine role (Rom 2:16; 2 Cor 5:10; cf. Acts 17:31). One finds a similar view in the Fourth Gospel. Though John sometimes speaks of those who do not believe in Jesus as already condemned (John 3:17-18), at other times he refers to a future judgment in which Jesus judges in union with the Father (John 5:26-29; 12:47-48).

The Synoptic Gospels, drawing on the apocalyptic vision of the Son of Man in Daniel 7:13, represent Jesus as "'the Son of Man coming in the clouds' with great power and glory" (Mark 13:26). Mark's gospel, written during a time of real or impending persecution, sets the coming of the Son of Man in an apocalyptic context, with persecutions, cosmic disturbances, and false messiahs all taking place before this generation passes away (Mark 13:9-31). Luke relates it to a more distant coming of the kingdom of God (Luke 21:31). But neither speaks here of judgment or punishment. That comes from Matthew, who introduces the traditional view of the Son of Man coming with angels and a trumpet blast (Matt 24:31), sitting before the assembled nations upon his throne, and separating the sheep from the goats (Matt 25:31-32).

For many evangelical Christians, the imminent Second Coming of Christ is a central doctrine, taken quite literally. It is often included among the five fundamentals, along with the inerrancy and sufficiency of the Bible, the virgin birth of Christ, the doctrine of substitutionary atonement, and bodily resurrection. Many look forward to Christ coming again visibly as ruler and judge. However, they are widely divided when it comes to describing how the Second Coming should be understood and when it will take place. The result is a proliferation of apocalyptic, millennial, and rapture theologies, most of them quite literalist in their interpretation of the Scripture. Because of its influence on American Christianity, it is important to consider evangelical Second Coming theology briefly here.

Millennialism

Millennial theology, rooted in Revelation 20, anticipates a thousand-year period in which Satan, his power broken, will be confined in the abyss and the just—those who have been saved—will reign with Christ, though it has been diversely understood. Amillennialism, no longer very popular, represents a less literal approach. It sees a thousand years as symbolic; the "millennium" is already underway since Christ has conquered Satan. When he comes again at the end of time the just will enter heaven, the wicked will be condemned to hell, and the earth will be destroyed by fire (2 Pet 2).

Premillennialism is very popular with fundamentalist Christians. It hopes for the conversion of the entire human race, including the Jews, which will inaugurate a millennium of righteousness and peace that will precede the Second Coming, resurrection of the dead, and last judgment. But it is incredibly diverse in the way it is imagined. While some premillennialists see the prophetic texts as more symbolic, most follow a "dispensationalist" theory which sees biblical significance in current world events such as the reestablishment of the nation of Israel and look forward to the "Rapture," when Christ will supernaturally remove those who have been saved from the earth, catching them up in the clouds "to meet the Lord in the air" (1 Thess 4:17; Matt 24:39-41), delivering them from the coming tribulation that will herald the end times.

There are again many different views of how and when the Rapture will take place. Pre-tribulation theology looks forward to the Rapture happening a thousand years before the Second Coming of Christ and the final judgments, ushering in a millennial reign of the just. In this camp are about one-third of America's thirty to forty million evangelicals who are unquestioning in their political support for the nation of Israel because they believe that according to the Bible, the Jews must return to the land of Israel before Christ can come again.[7] It is also popular with Seventh

---

[7] See Timothy P. Weber, *On the Road to Armageddon: How Evangelicals Became Israel's Best Friend* (Grand Rapids, MI: Baker Academic, 2004).

Day Adventists, Jehovah's Witnesses, and Pentecostals, and includes among its advocates Hal Lindsey, author of *The Late, Great Planet Earth*, as well as Tim LaHaye and Jerry Jenkins, authors of the very popular *Left Behind* series. Many fundamentalists believe that Catholics, whom they do not consider to be true Christians, will be among those "left behind." Other dispensationalist views include Post-Tribulation Rapture, Partial Rapture Premillennialism, Pre-Wrath Rapture, and so on.

If you are confused with all these theories, don't be surprised. The trouble with evangelical Second Coming theology is that the New Testament does not offer a single view of how God's salvation will be realized in its fullness, as is evident from the different views we have considered. Luke Timothy Johnson contrasts fundamentalists who in the name of the truth of Scripture continue to "fret about the rapture" and see signs of Armageddon in contemporary events with so many modern Christians who have so bought into Enlightenment reason that they "do not appreciate the importance of the conviction that God judges the world in Christ. They maintain an Enlightenment conviction that judgment is bad for religion."[8] But neither fundamentalists nor modernists get it right.

Judgment and Punishment

One does not have to believe literally in heaven and hell as places or even imagine God as personally handing out eternal punishment in order to accept the truth that each of us is responsible for our ultimate destiny. Pope John Paul II stressed this when he taught that hell was "not a punishment imposed externally by God but a development of premises already set by people in this life." Nor was hell a place; rather "hell indicates the state of those who freely and definitively separate themselves from God, the source of all life and joy."[9] The Pope's purpose was to emphasize the infinite goodness and compassion of God, who offers all people the grace of salvation, though each must ultimately accept or reject that gift.

As Augustine taught long ago, the deepest longing of the human heart is for union with God: "Our hearts are made for you O God, and they will not rest until they rest in you" (*Confessions* 1.1). Biblical symbols for

[8] Luke Timothy Johnson, *The Creed: What Christians Believe and Why it Matters* (New York: Doubleday, 2004) 202.

[9] Pope John Paul II, General Audience, July 28, 1999; cf. *Catechism of the Catholic Church*, no. 1033; numerous fundamentalist websites have condemned the Pope to hell himself for his teaching.

hell, among them the "pool of fire" and "the second death" (Rev 20:14) and "the penalty of eternal ruin, separated from the presence of the Lord" (2 Thess 1:9) underline the burden and the privilege of human freedom. God offers us the grace of salvation through Christ Jesus; but we can close ourselves to God's love. The choice is ours.

Thus God does not "punish" us for our sins. God does not "allow" attacks such as those on the World Trade Center and the Pentagon because of abortionists, feminists, gays, lesbians, and the ACLU, as Jerry Falwell and Pat Robertson suggested shortly after 9/11. God does not send AIDS or natural disasters like the 2004 tsunami off the coast of Indonesia as punishments. Our sins bring their own destructive consequences in their wake. They are evil, not because God has forbidden certain actions, but because to lie, cheat, steal, exploit others, or use violence against them introduces injustice, alienation, hatred, and more violence into our world. Sin injures those whom God loves, including ourselves. If we reject God's love, God respects our freedom. God cannot make us love him, for our love too is a gift. To die without a relationship with God is literally hell; we have excluded God from our life.

Conclusion

The language to express the first disciples' conviction that the Jesus who was crucified continued to live among them in a new way developed gradually. But from the beginning, they understood the Resurrection as God's vindication of Jesus and as his victory over sin and death. Jesus had gone down to the abode of the dead and had been raised up; death's power was broken. Jesus was now enthroned as Lord at God's right hand. Thus Paul could rejoice,

> Death is swallowed up in victory.
> Where, O death, is your victory?
> Where, O death, is your sting?
>   (1 Cor 15:55)

John constantly emphasizes Jesus' union with the Father in his gospel: "My food is to do the will of the one who sent me" (John 4:34), "I cannot do anything on my own" (John 5:30), for "The Father and I are one" (John 10:11). What John expresses theologically Jesus lived out existentially, even on the cross. When God seemed most distant from him in his agony and abandonment, he clung to the One he called Abba nonetheless.

In spite of the injustice, hatred, and violence he experienced in this extreme moment, he refused to give in to the demonic, forgiving those who persecuted him even from the cross (Luke 23:34). In dying as God's beloved Son with his relationship to God unbroken, he showed us the way, proving for us that God's love is stronger than death. Jesus' victory is ours. Death is not the end, but only a transition to the fullness of life with the God who fashioned us and offers us the gift of everlasting life.

The Second Coming of Christ is the symbol of his return to gather his own to himself. How that will happen remains a mystery. While many fundamentalists get lost in millennial visions, others today do not recognize that each of us must one day give an account of our stewardship. If we strive to live as disciples of Jesus we should, like the early Christians, await his coming for us with hope and joy.

The Holy Spirit

Chapter 10

"I believe in the Holy Spirit"

The third article of the Apostles' Creed is on the nature and work of the Holy Spirit. Though the New Testament speaks of God as Father, Jesus as Son, and of the Spirit, the doctrine of the Trinity itself does not appear in the New Testament. The divinity of the Holy Spirit was formally defined by the Council of Constantinople in 381, which added to Nicaea's confession of belief in the Holy Spirit the familiar "the Lord and Giver of life, who proceeds from the Father, who together with the Father and Son is adored and glorified, who spoke through the prophets" (DS 150). Since only God is to be worshiped, including the Spirit here with the Father and the Son is to acknowledge the Spirit's divinity.

If in the New Testament the Spirit is a symbol chiefly for God's active presence in the church and in the lives of believers, by the time the Apostles' Creed took on its final shape, the third article on the Holy Spirit was understood in light of the church's developed doctrine of the Trinity. As evidence of this, J. N. D. Kelly quotes Rufinus' commentary (404 CE): "with the mention of the Holy Spirit the mystery of the Trinity is completed."[1] However, the story of the development of the church's doctrine of the Trinity is complex.

The Holy Spirit

The Hebrew word *rûach* can mean breath, wind, principle of life, or spirit, depending on the context. It connotes an active force, something

---

[1] J. N. D. Kelly, *Early Christian Creeds* (New York: Longman, 1972) 383–84; *Commentarium in symbolum apostolorum* 33.

that animates and quickens. The Greek word *pneuma* is similar. In the Old Testament the "spirit" personifies God's creative presence and activity. Thus spirit or "a mighty wind" (NAB) hovers over the primordial waters before God creates the heavens and the earth (Gen 1:2; cf. Ps 104:29-30). The spirit empowers the prophets to speak God's word (Isa 11:2; 42:1) and is imparted to those chosen for some special task (Gen 41:38; Num 11:17; Judg 3:10). A rare usage in Isaiah 63:10 speaks of Yahweh's "holy spirit." An outpouring of the spirit is promised for the messianic age (Isa 44:3; Ezek 11:19; 32:15), even "upon all mankind" (Joel 3:1), which Paul sees as having been fulfilled through Christ Jesus, extending the blessing of Abraham to the Gentiles (Gal 3:14; cf. Acts 2:17-18).

The Spirit of God is active throughout the life of Jesus. He is conceived through the Holy Spirit (Matt 1:20; Luke 1:35), receives the Spirit at his baptism (Mark 1:10), is led by the Spirit into the wilderness (Luke 4:1), and undertakes his ministry in the power of the Spirit (Luke 4:18-19). Luke especially emphasizes the role of the Spirit in the life of Jesus.

In the New Testament "Spirit" and "grace" are practically synonymous terms for God's life in us. For Paul especially, the Spirit is the animating principle or power of life in the church. He speaks of "the Spirit of God" or "the Spirit of Christ" or simply "the Spirit" (Rom 8:9-11) to indicate how the risen Christ is present and active in the community. Elsewhere he says that Christ, the "new Adam," has become "a life-giving spirit" (1 Cor 15:45). The church is the temple or household of God, the "dwelling place of God in the Spirit" (Eph 2:19-22; cf. 1 Cor 3:16), for the Spirit dwells in the community of the disciples of Jesus, empowering them, creating the church.

Thus to be "in Christ" is to have new life "in the Spirit" which enables us to know God's love poured into our hearts (Rom 5:5), to call on God as *Abba* (Rom 8:15), and to confess Jesus as Lord (1 Cor 12:3). The Spirit unites those baptized into one body in Christ (1 Cor 12:13) and is the source of the church's charismatic structure and its ministry (1 Cor 12). The Spirit's presence can be recognized in our affectivity; the "fruit of the Spirit" is "love, joy, peace, patience, kindness, generosity, faithfulness, gentleness, self-control" (Gal 5:22). But there are also passages in Paul that describe the Spirit acting in the way that a person does. The Spirit "scrutinizes . . . the depths of God" (1 Cor 2:10), teaches (1 Cor 2:13), leads or guides (Rom 8:14; Gal 5:18), and intercedes for those led by the Spirit of God (Rom 8:26).

In the Fourth Gospel the personal character of the Spirit is more evident. The Spirit, called the Advocate (*paraklētos*), serves to unite the disciples with Jesus and the Father. Jesus asks the Father to send "another Advocate to be with [the disciples] always, the Spirit of truth" (John 14:16-17). "On that day you will realize that I am in my Father and you are in me and I in you" (John 14:20; cf. 16:5-15). "The Advocate, the holy Spirit . . . will teach you everything and remind you of all that [I] told you" (John 14:25). The Fourth Gospel presents the church as a community of disciples guided by the Spirit; it lacks the emphasis on emerging structures of authority and church office that one finds in other contemporary or even earlier New Testament documents. The commissioning of Peter as shepherd of the flock in the Johannine Appendix (John 21:15-17) is understood by many scholars as recommending to the Johannine Christians the presbyteral-episcopal structure emerging in the other churches.[2]

Trinitarian Formulas

From very early on there are hints of the threefold dimension of the divine life in which the believers share. Various triadic formulas speak of God's salvation or life in Christ and with the Spirit (2 Cor 1:21-22; Eph 1:13-14; 4:4-6). Paul uses one to conclude his second letter to the Corinthians: "The grace of the Lord Jesus Christ and the love of God and the fellowship [*koinōnia*] of the holy Spirit be with all of you" (2 Cor 13:13); today this blessing is used as a greeting in the liturgy. The church's baptismal formula comes from Matthew 28:19, with the risen Christ's instruction to baptize "in the name of the Father, and of the Son, and of the holy Spirit." Both are more properly trinitarian in form, both associate the Spirit with the Father and the Son. So does Paul's language grounding the gifts, ministries, and works of the community in God: "There are different kinds of spiritual gifts but the same Spirit; there are different forms of service but the same Lord; there are different workings but the same God who produces all of them in everyone" (1 Cor 12:4-5). There is a mutuality between the missions of Christ and the Spirit; in Kilian McDonnell's words, "The Holy Spirit is the point of entry into history and the Church in one direction, and, in another, into the Christological and Trinitarian mysteries."[3]

---

[2] For example, Raymond E. Brown, *The Community of the Beloved Disciple* (New York: Paulist Press, 1979) 162.

[3] Kilian McDonnell, "A Trinitarian Theology of the Holy Spirit?" *Theological Studies* 46/2 (1985) 226.

The Trinity

If one does not find the *doctrine* of the Trinity in the New Testament, "there is a definite binitarian or trinitarian pattern to salvation history: God redeems through Christ in the power of the Holy Spirit."[4] Contemporary theologians often distinguish between the "economic Trinity," God's self-manifestation in history as Father, Son, and Spirit, and the "immanent Trinity," God *in se*, a distinction rooted in the ancient terms *oikonomia* and *theologia*. Karl Rahner insists on the fundamental unity of the two concepts.[5]

According to Catherine LaCugna, in the first three centuries of the church the theological focus was on the *oikonomia*, a Greek word used for God's plan of salvation (Col 1:25; Eph 1:9-10) which revealed the one God or Father in the incarnation of the Son and the sending of the Holy Spirit. In other words, the *oikonomia* referred to God's self-revelation in the divine saving work in history. We come to know the Father through the Son and in the Holy Spirit.

While the Lordship of Jesus confessed by the early Christians implied the divine status of Jesus as well as God's presence and action through the Spirit, the focus was on God's saving work in history, not on the inner life of God, or *theologia*, as it was increasingly referred to after Nicaea. The Greek word *theologia* meant literally "words about God," thus to speak about God and things divine.

The liturgical practice of the church in the pre-Nicene period influenced its developing christological and trinitarian doctrines considerably. In the earliest Christian worship Jesus was invoked directly. He was *confessed* as Lord at baptism (Rom 10:8-13), *invoked* as Lord in the Christian assembly (1 Cor 16:22), *worshiped* as Lord by Christians (Phil 2:5-11), and *prayed to* for assistance in times of need (Acts 7:59; 2 Cor 12:8).[6] In the later pre-Nicene period the thanksgiving and prayer of the church was addressed to the Father *in the name of* the Lord Jesus Christ (Eph 5:20; Col 3:17; cf. 1 Cor 1:4) or *through* him (Rom 1:8; 16:27; 1 Cor 15:57). In his treatise *On Prayer* (232), Origen advised that all prayers be ended "by praising the Father through Jesus Christ in the Holy Spirit," reflecting the practice of his day.

---

[4] Catherine Mowry LaCugna, *God For Us: The Trinity and Christian Life* (Harper-SanFrancisco, 1991) 22.

[5] Karl Rahner, *The Trinity* (New York: Herder and Herder, 1970) 21.

[6] Geoffrey Wainwright, *Doxology: The Praise of God in Worship, Doctrine, and Life* (New York: Oxford University Press, 1980) 47–48 at 47.

Thus the church's interest in the first three centuries was primarily soteriological (concerned with our salvation), not ontological (concerned with God's inner life, God *in se*). But this changed considerably after Nicaea (325) and the struggle with Arianism. As we saw earlier, Arius' doctrine reflected a Hellenistic understanding of the transcendent divinity, reducing the Son to a lesser divine being, an intermediary between the unbegotten, impassible God and the world of change. The church's liturgical pattern, praying to the Father through the Son, reinforced Arius' impression that Jesus Christ was less than God. In response to the challenge of Arianism, the bishops assembled at Nicaea confessed in what became the Nicene Creed that Jesus was "of the same substance as" or "one in being with" (*homoousios*) the Father, as we have seen.

But Nicaea's teaching was received only gradually, and the Arian theology did not immediately fade away, particularly in the East. To counteract this, the focus shifted in the post-Nicene period considerably from the divine *oikonomia* to *theologia*, the inner life of God, with a growing rupture between the two. Liturgically, prayers addressed directly to Christ outside the eucharistic prayer appeared, while the liturgy was addressed to God or the Father *through* Christ *in* the Holy Spirit. As LaCugna notes, with the growing anti-Arian emphasis on the divinity of Jesus, there was less emphasis on his role as mediator and high priest in his humanity (cf. Heb 4:14-16). Jesus as the one who unites us to God "becomes infinitely distant from us, taking his place 'at the right hand of the Father' not as exalted Lord but as preexistent Christ."[7] The result was a diminished consciousness of the triumph of the incarnate Word who remains joined to us in his humanity.

Some of those popularly known as Semi-Arians in the post-Nicaean period also denied the divinity of the Holy Spirit. Thus they were known as the *Pneumatomachoi*, "Enemies of the Spirit," or sometimes as Macedonians, after their leader, Macedonius, bishop of Constantinople (d. after 360). The doctrine of the *Pneumatomachoi* was opposed by the three great Cappadocians, Basil the Great (330–379), Gregory of Nyssa (335–394), and Gregory of Nazianzus (c. 329–389). It was Gregory of Nazianzus who brought the Cappadocian theology to the Council of Constantinople (381), playing an important role in its confession of the divinity of the Holy Spirit as "the Lord and Giver of life, who proceeds from the Father, who together with the Father and Son is adored and glorified."

---

[7] LaCugna, *God for Us*, 126.

This language became the language of the Nicene-Constantinopolitan Creed.

The Filioque Controversy

An enduring source of controversy between the churches of the East and West was the addition of the so-called *"filioque"* clause to the Creed by the West in the eleventh century. The 381 Creed had confessed that the Spirit proceeds "from the Father." There were some differences of emphasis between the language of the East and the West. The West followed the concept that the Spirit emanates principally (*principaliter*) from the Father. Some Latin theologians spoke of a "double procession," among them Ambrose (d. 397), Jerome (d. 420), and Augustine (d. 430). Using the *filioque* clause to express the idea that the Spirit proceeded from the Father "and the Son" (*filioque*) seems to have been first introduced into the Creed by the Third Council of Toledo in 589, a local council. The efforts of Charlemagne to make use of the *filioque* standard in the liturgy of the West were resisted by several popes out of sensitivity to the East. It was not generally used in Rome until the mid-eleventh century.

While the dispute reflects in part the different theologies of the East and West, with the East concerned to safeguard the monarchy of the Father as origin and source of the Son and the Spirit, the West stressed that from the perspective of the *oikonomia* the Spirit is the Spirit of both the Father and the Son. As LaCugna says, "It is impossible to think or speak of the Spirit except as the Spirit-of. The Holy Spirit is the Spirit of God, Spirit of Christ, Spirit of the Christian community."[8] Gerald O'Collins makes a similar point. The East was concerned about what many saw as the subordination of the Spirit to the Son in Christian life, and of pneumatology to christology in theology.[9] And it needs to be said that pneumatology has not always been given its proper place in the Western Church.

But at the heart of the Eastern objection is the fact that the *filioque* was added to the common creed unilaterally, without the consent of the East. Relations between the churches of the East and the West have been troubled by this to this day.

Walter Kasper, like other theologians, has suggested interpreting the *filioque* clause in the context of the common Creed of 381, with both sides

---

[8] LaCugna, *God for Us*, 298.

[9] Gerald O'Collins, *The Tripersonal God: Understanding and Interpreting the Trinity* (New York: Paulist Press, 1999) 140.

renewing their trinitarian theology. If Catholics could emphasize that the Spirit *principaliter* emanates from the Father (monarchy), the East might better address the relationship between the Son and the Spirit, with the implication of a relational trinitarian ontology so important for a *communio*-ecclesiology. The Catholic Church after thorough pastoral preparation could use the original wording of the Creed in its liturgy for the sake of unity and peace, without renouncing what it intends to affirm and without either side attempting to impose its language on the other.[10] Noting the differences in theological expression, the *Catechism of the Catholic Church* states: "This legitimate complementarity, provided it does not become rigid, does not affect the identity of faith in the reality of the same mystery confessed" (no. 248).

Conclusion

During his ministry Jesus was accused by the scribes of being possessed: "By the prince of demons he drives out demons." In response he told them that "all sins and all blasphemies that people utter will be forgiven them. But whoever blasphemes against the holy Spirit will never have forgiveness, but is guilty of an everlasting sin" (Mark 3:28-29).

What is this sin against the Holy Spirit that cannot be forgiven? It means first of all, attributing to Satan what is obviously the work of the Spirit. At the same time, it means that obstinacy and hardness of heart that refuses to acknowledge what is obviously good, that cannot recognize the Spirit's work because one's own works are evil. Those who close themselves to the Spirit will remain in their blindness and their sin. This is the sin that in the words of Scripture cannot be forgiven.

Though the church came to grasp the divinity of the Spirit only gradually, its vivifying role in the community was evident from the beginning. The Christians of the first three centuries had a vivid sense of the mediatory role of the risen Christ who in his glorified humanity pleads our cause before God. The doctrine of the Trinity is one of the great achievements of the early church, formulating the early Christians' sense of our communion with God through Christ in the Spirit. But the increasing emphasis on God's inner life, largely a result of the church's long struggle with Arianism, resulted in a less vivid experience of the Spirit's power.

[10] Walter Kasper, *That They May All be One: The Call to Unity Today* (London: Burns and Oates, 2004) 112–15.

The doctrine of the Holy Spirit is an expression of our share in the divine life, the inner life of God revealed in Jesus and bringing us new life in the Holy Spirit. That divine life must in some way become evident in our experience.

The theology and liturgy of Eastern Christianity to this day is more pneumatological than that of the West. If Western theology seems abstract and theoretical to many, the remarkable growth of Pentecostal Christianity in our time owes much of its success to a renewed sense of the vital power of the Spirit within the Christian community. Pentecostalism is experiential. Renato Poblete, a Chilean Jesuit, attributes the effectiveness of the Pentecostals in Latin America to their emphasis on a subjective experience of God, a subjective element that Western theology has too often lost sight of.[11]

I first experienced the power of Pentecostal Christianity several nights before I was ordained when I attended for the first time a liturgy celebrated with a Catholic charismatic community on our campus. Rich in charismatic preaching, prophecy, singing in tongues, prayers for healing, and a sheer exuberance in the Spirit, it was unlike any liturgy I had ever experienced. I wondered if I was really in a Catholic Church! The charismatic renewal within Catholicism and other mainline churches has helped many to experience the power of the Spirit. They have come to a more affective faith, become more comfortable with spontaneous prayer and emotion in worship, and found a more personal experience of the Spirit. Today the charismatic movement is particularly strong among Hispanic Catholics; indeed, as Gastón Espinosa notes, the Catholic Charismatic movement is one of the largest and fastest growing movements in both Latin America and the United States today.[12]

But these more dramatic experiences of the Spirit are not the only expressions of our share in the divine life. We should experience God's life within us. Christianity has a rich tradition of prayer, from St. Paul who spoke guardedly of his own mystical experience (2 Cor 12:1-4), through the great mystics and teachers of the Christian tradition. St. Teresa of Avila described the "Prayer of Quiet," a type of infused prayer in which

[11] Renato Poblete, "The Catholic Church and Latin America's Pentecostals," *Origins* 27/43 (1998) 719–20.

[12] Gastón Espinosa, "The Impact of Pluralism on Trends in Latin American and U.S. Latino Religions and Society," *Perspectivas*, Hispanic Theological Initiative Occasional Paper Series, Issue Seven (Fall 2003) 16.

our senses are stilled and our attention remains focused on God, in her book *The Way of Perfection*.

> I still want to describe this prayer of quiet to you in the way that I have heard it explained and as the Lord has been pleased to teach it to me. . . . This is a supernatural state and however hard we try, we cannot acquire it by ourselves. . . . The faculties are stilled and have no wish to move, for any movement they make seems to hinder the soul from loving God. They are not completely lost, however, since two of them are free and they can realize in whose presence they are. It is the will that is captive now. . . . The intellect tries to occupy itself with only one thing, and the memory has no desire to busy itself with more. They both see that this is the one thing necessary; anything else will cause them to be disturbed. (chap. 31)

Teresa's contemporary and fellow Carmelite St. John of the Cross described a similar contemplation he called acquired, which one could strive for with the help of divine grace. Both represent more passive forms of prayer, focused on God who remains in our hearts and is grasped in faith.

St. Ignatius of Loyola's gift to the church was his *Spiritual Exercises*, a series of meditations and contemplations of the gospel mysteries which help the retreatant discover in his or her own life the presence of God and movements of the Spirit. Based on the principle that God works directly on the person at prayer, his treatment of the discernment of spirits, to see how one is being moved, is particularly important.

At the end of the *Spiritual Exercises*, Ignatius proposes an exercise called the *Contemplatio ad Amorem*, the Contemplation for Obtaining Love, with four points for the retreatant's consideration. First, he invites the retreatant to consider the many gifts he or she has received from God, including the gifts of creation and redemption, and the many gifts particular to each person. Second, he or she should consider how God dwells in these gifts, giving them according to their kind of being, life, sensation, and understanding. Third, he or she should reflect on how God is "working" or "laboring" in these gifts, preserving them in being, giving them life and sensation. Finally, he suggests that the retreatant consider how these gifts descend from above and reflect in different ways the goodness, justice, and mercy of their creator, just as the rays of light descend from the brilliance of the sun.

From this contemplation comes the idea of "finding God in all things," a stance towards life and one's experience basic to Ignatian spirituality. But it is important to note that one doesn't gain this graced vision simply by looking. It is rooted in the experience of having made the *Spiritual Exercises*. It presumes that one has received the grace of the First Week, that deep awareness that our sins have been forgiven and that we are loved and cherished by God. It presumes that one has pondered the meditations on the Call of the Earthly King and the Two Standards and has responded generously, seeking to come to know Christ our Lord by meditating on the mysteries of his life. It means that one has prayed through the mystery of the passion of Christ in the Third Week, accompanying Jesus in his abandonment, sharing in his sorrow and pain, and finally, rejoicing with the disciples in contemplating the appearances of the risen Lord in the Fourth Week. It is this experience of knowing oneself as forgiven, redeemed, loved, called, and blessed that opens the eyes of one's soul and spirit to the mystery of God's ubiquity, that enables one to recognize God's presence in all the events and circumstances of one's life.

Today many outside the monastic and religious life have become familiar with contemplative prayer. Trappist monk Thomas Merton brought it to the attention of many in his writings, particularly his wonderful book, *New Seeds of Contemplation*.[13] Others have learned contemplative prayer from contemporary teachers like Basil Pennington, Thomas Keating, and Henri Nouwen. Such prayer helps us experience the nearness of the God who gives us a share in the divine life, who is closer to us than we are to ourselves, the God who has poured into our hearts the Holy Spirit of adoption through whom we too can cry, "*Abba*, Father" (Rom 8:14-15).

---

[13] Thomas Merton, *New Seeds of Contemplation* (Norfolk, CT: New Directions, 1961).

Chapter 11

"The holy catholic Church"

The Creed moves easily from belief in the Holy Spirit to belief in the holy catholic church, for the Spirit's work in gathering disciples becomes visible in the community called church. The church exists from the time of the Resurrection, when the disciples, scattered by the trauma of the crucifixion, were gathered together again by their Easter experience and experienced the outpouring of the Spirit. Indeed the Greek word for church, *ekklēsia*, means literally those called out or called together, thus assembly. It was used in the Septuagint to translate the Hebrew *kehal*, as in *kehal Yahweh* or assembly of the Lord (cf. Num 16:3; Deut 23:2).

Though the word *ekklēsia* does not appear in the gospels, with the exception of two passages in Matthew (16:18; 18:17), one finds it used widely in the rest of the New Testament, in the Pauline and Deutero-pauline letters (sixty-five times), the Acts of the Apostles (twenty-three times), 3 John (vv. 6, 9, 10), Revelation (over twenty times), and James (5:14). Among New Testament metaphors for church three are particularly significant. "People of God" shows the continuity of the church with God's revelation to Israel. "Body of Christ" is used by Paul to describe the community united by baptism (1 Cor 12:12-13) and the Lord's Supper with the risen Jesus and with each other (1 Cor 10:16-17). "Temple of the Spirit" draws together various New Testament descriptions of the Christian community as guided by the Spirit; it is in Paul's words "the household of God . . . a temple sacred in the Lord . . . a dwelling place of God in the Spirit (Eph 2:19-22; cf. 1 Tim 3:15). Similar expressions for this gathering of the disciples of Jesus include "sheep-fold" (John 10:1 ff.) and "synagogue" (Jas 2:2). The church mediates God's salvation.

The Church

The church we profess as ours has its roots in the Jesus movement, the group of men and women called together by Jesus as his disciples to share in his own mission to Israel. Recognizable in the gospels, the disciples constituted a unique family, based not on clan, kinship, or patriarchy, but on doing the will of God (Mark 3:33-35). While the historical Jesus did not "found" the church, in the sense of giving it a structure and constitution, he clearly established its foundations and gave it the sacraments of baptism and Eucharist. In gathering his disciples and placing at their center "the Twelve," symbolizing the twelve tribes of Israel, with Peter foremost among them as a spokesman, and in giving them a share in his own ministry (Mark 6:7-13; Luke 10:2-12), his movement represented a renewed or eschatological Israel.

Thus the first Christians were all Jews who continued to see themselves as part of Judaism. As Acts tells us, "Every day they devoted themselves to meeting together in the temple area and to breaking bread in their homes" (Acts 2:46). As these first Christians, the apostles, prophets, and evangelists (cf. Eph 4:11), spread the good news of God's grace revealed in the death and resurrection of Jesus, they rapidly established churches from Jerusalem to Rome. But tensions developed between the synagogue and the church as Christianity spread and the Jewish community, under the leadership of the Pharisees, reorganized its life in the period after the destruction of the temple and the loss of the priesthood. The expulsion or excommunication of the Christian Jews from the synagogue, somewhere around the year 90, is reflected in some of the "anti-Jewish" language in the Gospel of Matthew (23:1-36) and in references to being put out of the synagogue for confessing Jesus as messiah and persecutions in John (9:22; 12:42; 16:2).

In the first generations the different Christian communities varied considerably in theology as well as ministerial structure and vocabulary, reflecting the different religious and cultural backgrounds of their missionary founders—Jewish Christian, Hellenistic, Pauline, Johannine, Apocalyptic, and "early Catholic," the last a term used pejoratively by some Protestant scholars for what they see as an attempt to "bind" the

Spirit to an institutionalized church office.[1] Still these different churches were united from the beginning by certain fundamental beliefs; these included their experience of God's saving power in the exalted Christ; an awareness of being in continuity with Israel, apostolicity, in the sense of receiving the tradition from the Twelve and the other apostles, and the practice of baptism and the Eucharist. They were able to live with considerable diversity and still remain in communion (*koinōnia*) with each other.[2]

While Paul generally used the word *ekklēsia* for the local church, in Ephesians and Colossians the word most often refers to the whole or universal church. The laying-on of hands had emerged by the end of the first century as a ritual sign for appointment to office (1 Tim 5:22; 2 Tim 1:6). The first clear attempt to link eucharistic presidency with church leadership appears in Ignatius of Antioch around 110 (*Smyrneans* 8:1).[3] By the early second century the structures of the various communities had begun to coalesce in what would be known as the Catholic Church. The threefold structure of a bishop, surrounded by presbyters and assisted by deacons was in place at Antioch and some other churches by 110, and by the end of the second century present virtually throughout the church. These ritual and structural developments represented a process of "institutionalization" which would enable the church to survive as it spread throughout the Greco-Roman world. A less happy effect of these developments was the loss of the sense for the rich diversity of charisms present among the faithful, so recognizable in Paul's letters (1 Cor 12–14; Rom 12:3-8), as well as their openness to women in missionary and ministerial roles.

By the third century the scattered communities of the New Testament period had become a "Great Church," reaching from Africa to Spain, with the church of Rome increasingly recognized as the center of the communion. The church has continued to grow and change in every

---

[1] See Ernst Käsemann, "Paul and Early Catholicism," in his *New Testament Questions of Today* (London: SCM Press, 1969) 236–51; see also Raymond E. Brown, *The Churches the Apostles Left Behind* (New York: Paulist Press, 1984).

[2] Thomas P. Rausch, *Towards a Truly Catholic Church* (Collegeville, MN: Liturgical Press, 2005) 2–4.

[3] Luke's linking Jesus' role as servant with that of the apostles at the Last Supper can also be seen as an effort to link church leaders with eucharistic presidency; see Edward Schillebeeckx, *Jesus: An Experiment in Christology* (New York: Seabury Press, 1979) 304.

age, adopting cultural forms and time-conditioned political structures to a degree it has rarely acknowledged. The conciliar movement in the fifteenth century attempted to give the church a constitutional structure that balanced the primacy of the bishop of Rome with the conciliar authority of all the bishops. But that was just a moment against the background of a papal absolutism that had been developing since the eleventh century and reached its apogee with the definition of papal primacy and infallibility by the First Vatican Council (1870). Vatican II (1962–65) went a considerable way towards restoring the collegial character of the church of the first millennium, though that vision of how church authority should function has not always been honored in the post-conciliar period.

The Marks of the Church

While the Apostles' Creed confesses belief simply in "the holy catholic church," the First Council of Constantinople in 381 added a more complex phrase that speaks of "one, holy, catholic and apostolic church," four descriptors which would come to be known as the marks of the church.

The Church is One

The church is one, for all were baptized into one body and given to drink of one Spirit (1 Cor 12:13). Unity is the Spirit's gift. The church is one body in Christ, for the many disciples, partaking of the one loaf, are united by their communion in the body and the blood of Christ (1 Cor 10:16-17). Unity does not mean uniformity; it can coexist with considerable diversity. What unity excludes is disharmony, divisiveness, and sectarianism. Yet the church today is de facto divided, existing as separate denominations no longer in communion with each other, divisions stemming from theological differences, cultural and political estrangement, and an unwillingness to carry out needed reforms.

The Catholic Church claims a unity visibly expressed by the bonds of a common faith, sacraments, ecclesiastical government, and communion, including communion with the Supreme Pontiff (LG 14). The particular churches are united by the bonds of communion that join their bishops with each other and with the Bishop of Rome, visible source of the unity of the bishops. "In and from such individual churches there comes into being the one and only Catholic Church" (LG 23). Orthodox Christians see the local church as fully church, though some Orthodox theologians acknowledge that unity is more an abstract ideal than something that can be manifested in the real life of the church. Protestant churches generally distinguish between the visible church and the true, invisible church, or they see the unity of the visible church as being realized only in the eschatological future. Some Free Church theologians acknowledge that their ecclesiology "allows us to speak only of a plurality of churches rather than of the *one* church."[4]

The ecumenical movement, from its first beginnings at the World Missionary Conference at Edinburgh in 1910 that came to realize that divisions in the church impeded its evangelical mission, to its contemporary expressions in the World Council of Churches, the Pontifical Council for Promoting Christian Unity, and Christian Churches Together in the United States, has moved the different churches and ecclesial traditions from hostility and estrangement to in many cases mutual respect and cooperation. The ecclesial climate today is very different from what it was at the beginning of the twentieth century.

Still the goal of visible unity remains elusive. Tragically, it is easier to preserve unity than to restore it, once it has been lost. Too often the churches remain divided not just by theological and cultural differences, but sometimes by institutional inertia and a personal unwillingness to change that keeps the baptized from being a true "communion of saints," a "sacrament—a sign and instrument, that is, of communion with God and of the unity of the entire human race" (LG 1). As long as the church remains divided, its witness is diminished.

The Church is Holy

Baptismal creeds from the third century commonly asked, "Do you believe in the Holy Spirit, in the holy Church, and in the resurrection of the body?" (Hippolytus, *Apostolic Tradition* 21.17). The church is holy because of God's abiding presence; thus its holiness is derivative. The church is the People of God, the Body of Christ (1 Cor 12:27), "a dwelling place of God in the Spirit" (Eph 2:21-22), and it calls all the baptized to holiness of life (LG 5). The early New Testament documents refer to Christians as the holy ones or saints (*hagioi*; Rom 1:7; 12:13; 1 Cor 14:33; Phil 4:22). There have been great saints throughout the church's history, not just the ones we honor in our liturgy, art, and iconography, but countless millions remembered only by those who loved them or whose own

---

[4] Miroslav Volf, *After Our Likeness: The Church as the Image of the Trinity* (Grand Rapids, MI: William B. Eerdmans, 1998) 157.

lives were enriched by their example. The church is also holy because of God's holy gifts, the word of God (Jas 1:21), the church's ministry (2 Cor 5:18), the sacraments (1 Cor 6:11), and the Eucharist (1 Cor 11:27).

If the church is holy, it is also sinful, though official Catholicism is reluctant to use such language. It has had problems with authority since its earliest days. The gospels report the disciples arguing over who among them was the greatest (Mark 9:34; Luke 22:24). Paul found his own ministry disparaged by some at Corinth, overly impressed by those he refers to as the "superapostles" (2 Cor 11:5; 12:11). The author of the Johannine letters laments that Diotrephes, a leader in the church to whom he was writing, "loves to dominate" (3 John 9). Some of the Johannine communities, precisely because they were lacking strong leadership, seem to have moved later in the direction of Gnosticism.

The church at Corinth was still having problems two generations after Paul had written the Christians there; they had ejected the presbyters there from their office. In addressing this problem, a leader of the church of Rome known as Clement begins a long and sad history of jealousy in the story of God's people, running from Cain up to the "greatest and most righteous pillars of the Church" in his time, Peter and Paul. He even suggests that the death of Peter was due to the jealousy of other Christians (1 Clement 5:4). There have been compromised ministers in every age of the church, corrupt popes, venal bishops, unfaithful priests, as we know so well from the sexual abuse scandal in our own time. And there have been "nominal" Christians in every age of the church's life. Romano Guardini, one of the great twentieth-century theologians, is said to have observed, "The church is the cross on which Christ is crucified [again]."

The Church is Catholic

While the Old Roman Creed referred only to the "holy church," by the late fourth century the word "catholic" began to appear in Western creeds. It had first been used as a predicate for the church by St. Ignatius of Antioch (d. 110) as the New Testament period was coming to an end: "Wheresoever the bishop shall appear, there let the people be; even as where Jesus may be, there is the universal [*katholikē*] Church" (*Smyrneans* 8:2).[5] Ignatius' purpose here was to distinguish the local church or congregation under the bishop from the whole church under Christ.[6]

---

[5] J. B. Lightfoot, *The Apostolic Fathers* (Grand Rapids, MI: Baker Books, 1987) 84.

[6] J. N. D. Kelly, *Early Christian Creeds* (New York: Longman, 1972) 385.

The Greek *katholikē* originally meant whole or universal, but by the middle of the third century it was being used to distinguish "the great Church" from the rapidly growing heretical sects. Kelly quotes the martyr Pionius (250), who when asked by his judges, "To what church do you belong?" answered, "To the Catholic Church."[7] This distinguishing character of "catholic" was common up through the fourth century, especially when rival churches related to Arianism, Donatism, and other heresies were being established. Thus in a catechetical instruction Cyril of Jerusalem (d. 386) described the catholicity of the church as follows:

> The Church is called catholic then because it extends over all the world, from one end of the earth to the other; and because it teaches universally and completely one and all the doctrines which ought to come to men's knowledge, concerning things both visible and invisible, heavenly and earthly; and because it brings into subjection to godliness the whole race of mankind, governors and governed, learned and unlearned; and because it universally treats and heals the whole class of sins, which are committed by soul or body, and possesses in itself every form of virtue which is named, both in deeds and words, and in every kind of spiritual gifts. (Cat 18, 23)

In subsequent centuries the tendency grew to explain "catholic" in terms of "universal," without losing entirely the other meanings. Today many churches claim catholicity because the word "catholic" is confessed in the creeds, though they interpret it differently. Roman Catholics stress catholicity as universality. Orthodox Christians tend to argue that each local church as a eucharistic community is fully catholic, representing the one body of Christ in its totality and completeness. Though Luther substituted the world *christlich* (Christian) for catholic in the creed, Melanchthon and other Reformers claimed catholicity for their churches on the basis of their adherence to the teachings of the ancient, undivided church.

Today some evangelicals remain reluctant to use the word catholic and many Free Church commentators tend to reduce catholicity to an eschatological characteristic, to be realized only in the eschatological future when God will be "all in all" (Eph 1:10; 1 Cor 15:28). Others see it as describing the fullness of salvation in the individual church. Some traditions express their catholicity by belonging to communions or world

---

[7] Ibid.

confessional families such as the Anglican Communion, the Lutheran World Fellowship, or the World Alliance of Reformed Churches.

For Catholics, catholicity means being in communion with the communion of churches that constitutes the Catholic Church, a communion that is both sacramental and hierarchical and includes communion with the Bishop of Rome. Still, because of the divisions that remain among Christians, the Catholic Church acknowledges that "the church herself finds it more difficult to express in actual life her full catholicity in all its aspects" (UR 4).

The Church is Apostolic

The church is apostolic, founded on the apostles and prophets, with Christ Jesus himself as the capstone (Eph 2:20). The church of every age must be "apostolic," living in continuity with the church of the apostles and in fidelity to their teaching. This is known as apostolic succession. From the second century bishops were recognized as successors to the apostles, and witnesses such as Hegesippus (ca. 180), Irenaeus (d. ca. 200), and Tertullian (ca. 200) appealed to lists of bishops from churches that claimed apostolic foundation to show that they had preserved the apostolic tradition. The bishops personify the church's unity with her source; according to Joseph Ratzinger, now Pope Benedict XVI, this understanding of the apostolic succession belongs intrinsically to the church's structure.[8]

Today there are different understandings of apostolicity among the churches. The Anglican, Catholic, and Orthodox churches continue to emphasize apostolicity through the historic episcopal office. Protestant churches which lost the historic episcopate at the time of the Reformation follow Calvin (*Institutes* 4.2.2-3) in stressing apostolicity as conformity with the teaching of the apostles. Pentecostals stress succession in apostolic life, particularly in the charismatic gifts—tongues, prophecy, and healing powers—received through baptism in the Spirit.

The marks cannot be understood univocally, as though one church or tradition realized them fully. A church might claim a spiritual unity with other churches, but if that unity is nowhere expressed in real, visible relationships, its unity would be questionable. The holiness of a church should be evident in its reverence for the word and its celebra-

---

[8] Joseph Ratzinger, *Principles of Catholic Theology: Building Stones for a Fundamental Theology* (San Francisco: Ignatius Press, 1987) 194.

tion of the sacraments, as well as in the lives of its members; it should be expressed not just in external devotion but also in ethical living and concern for the poor. It would be difficult to see holiness in a church which did not welcome the poor or divided its eucharistic table on the basis of race. Catholicity does not mean simply full, but universal, in contrast to what is local or particular. It cannot be rightly understood without reference to communion with the whole or universal church. A church or tradition whose faith had departed significantly from the apostolic tradition, or which no longer celebrated baptism or the Eucharist would be deficient in apostolicity. Thus the marks stand as a challenge to all the churches.

Salvation Outside the Church?

If the church mediates God's salvation, can those outside the church be saved, or in evangelical terms, those who do not have a personal relationship with Jesus? The Second Vatican Council addressed this specifically, moving Catholic teaching forward on this issue.

The principle or axiom, "no salvation outside the Church" (*extra ecclesia nulla salus*) has a long history. Originally it referred to those who had separated themselves from the church through schism or heresy. By the time that most of the Roman Empire had become Christian, it began to be used for the minority that had not accepted the faith, including the Jews. What had been a warning to errant Christians now implied a judgment against those outside the church. Stressing the necessity of baptism, Augustine rejected the possibility of salvation for Jews, pagans, or even infants who died without baptism. John Chrysostom (d. 407), judging that the Jews had rejected Christ, used "some of the most offensive language about Jews to be found in Christian literature,"[9] though some modern scholars note that his remarks were directed primarily at the Judaizing Christians who were trying to live in both communities.[10]

Augustine was to influence the teachings of popes and councils down to modern times. For example, the Council of Florence (1442) taught that it "firmly believes, professes and preaches that all those who are outside

---

[9] See Francis A. Sullivan, *Salvation Outside the Church? Tracing the History of the Catholic Response* (New York: Paulist Press, 1992) 26.

[10] See Eugene J. Fisher (ed.), *Interwoven Destinies: Jews and Christian Through the Ages* (New York: Paulist, 1993).

the catholic church, not only pagans but also Jews or heretics and schismatics, cannot share in eternal life and will go into the everlasting fire which was prepared for the devil and his angels."[11]

At the same time another tradition began developing as early as Thomas Aquinas, who seems to have recognized an ignorance of Christ that was not culpable. But it was the so-called discovery of the "New World" of the Americas with its untold millions who had never heard the Gospel that led some Jesuits in Rome and Dominicans in Spain in the sixteenth and seventeenth centuries to conclude that salvation was possible for those who believed in God, even without explicit knowledge of Christ.[12] Pius IX repeated the traditional doctrine, teaching that no one could be saved outside of the apostolic Roman Church, but he also officially acknowledged for the first time that the traditional teaching applied only to those who were outside the church because of invincible ignorance, in other words, through no fault of their own. Those of us who were raised on the Baltimore Catechism remember that it taught three kinds of baptism, of water, blood, and desire, the last two of which are not baptism at all.

Thus even before the Second Vatican Council the church's perspective was broadening in regards to the axiom. The Council committed the church to a new posture towards other religions and acknowledged that those "outside" its boundaries could be saved. It taught that the church recognizes the Jewish people as "beloved for the sake of the fathers, for God never regrets his gifts or his call (see Rom 11:28-29)." The Muslims are also included in God's plan of salvation, for "they profess to hold the faith of Abraham, and together with us they adore the one, merciful God." The council taught officially that salvation is possible for them, and for others:

> Those who, through no fault of their own, do not know the Gospel of Christ or his church, but who nevertheless seek God with a sincere heart, and, moved by grace, try in their actions to do his will as they know it through the dictates of their conscience—these too may attain eternal salvation. Nor will divine providence deny the assistance necessary for salvation to those who, without any fault of theirs, have not yet arrived at an explicit knowledge of God, and who, not without grace, strive to lead a good life. (LG 16)

---

[11] Bull of Union with the Copts.
[12] Sullivan, *Salvation Outside the Church?* 98.

In recognizing a wideness in God's mercy, extending grace even to those who have not heard the Gospel, as well as acknowledging that the great religions of the world "often reflect a ray of that truth which enlightens all men and women" (NA 2), the council prepared the Catholic church for the dialogue with world religions that will be increasingly important in the twenty-first century. In fact, dialogue with those of other faiths becomes a genuinely religious event, undertaken with a reverence for the other and a respect for their religious traditions, for the Spirit of God may be present there. Vatican II's revision of the traditional axiom shows that the magisterium is one of God's gifts to the church. It is evidence that the church is a living community of faith that, assisted by the Spirit, can rethink aspects of its tradition and occasionally reformulate its doctrine.

Evangelical Christians continue to struggle with this issue. Many of them, locked into a biblical literalism, are not able to move beyond the traditional axiom, though they usually express it differently, denying the possibility of salvation for those who have not been "born again" through an explicit, personal relationship with Jesus. Some evangelicals misunderstand the Catholic position, arguing that Catholics teach universal salvation. But this is not the case. The council underlined the reality of sin, stressing that too often human beings "have exchanged the truth of God for a lie and served the creature rather than the Creator (see Rom 1:21 and 25)" (LG 16).

The council insisted that Christ is the fullness of God's truth (DV 2). The Catholic Church, the universal sacrament of salvation (LG 48), has been endowed with all divinely revealed truth (UR 3), a teaching underlined by the Congregation for the Doctrine of the Faith's declaration, *Dominus Iesus* (2000).[13]

Conclusion

The church is the community of the disciples of Jesus, continuing the movement Jesus began in his ministry. As early as 110 CE the church was called "catholic," meaning whole or full as opposed to what was partial, heretical, or sectarian, or universal as opposed to what was only local. By the end of the early third century the word catholic was being used to distinguish the true church from heretical or schismatic groups.

---

[13] "'*Dominus Iesus*': On the Unicity and Salvific Universality of Jesus Christ and the Church," *Origins* 30, no. 14 (2000) 210–19.

The "Catholic Church" has historically become the name of a particular Christian communion, perhaps the oldest institution in history. But it is larger than the Roman Catholic Church, as Eastern Rite Catholics—belonging to some twenty-two Eastern churches in communion with Rome—continue to insist. The Orthodox and Anglican churches can be said to belong to the Catholic tradition, as they share the episcopal and sacramental structure of the ancient church, and many Protestants and evangelicals claim catholicity as a mark or character of their churches, though they understand it differently.

What seems to many the impersonal institutionality of the church can be an obstacle to belief. Almost two thousand years old, patriarchal in its governing structure, jealous and protective of its authority, slow to change, the church often seems content to put its own institutional interests ahead of pastoral needs. Many see it as obstructionist, anti-modern, afraid of sex. It is often contemned by a liberal, secular culture which esteems self-expression as the highest value. The values of representative structures and participation in decision-making, so important to contemporary Americans, have rarely found expression in the church's official governance.

Still, it is precisely the church's papal-episcopal structure which has enabled it to endure for two millennia, balancing the local and the universal, the conciliar and the primatial in a communion which embraces diversity within a greater unity. Its institutionality is one of its greatest strengths, for being a Christian is more than simply believing in God or living an ethical life. One can't really be a Christian without the church. For many postmodern, secular people, this is difficult to grasp.

Our culture is radically individualistic. We like to argue that belonging to a religious community is not important, claiming a personal spirituality or one's own understanding of God. Partly this individualism reflects the Protestant roots of American culture, a country founded by religious sectarians who, because they were persecuted in the old country, exalted freedom of conscience against any authority, religious or civil. Partly it reflects the individualistic doctrine of salvation of evangelical Protestantism, "the near exclusive focus on the relation between Jesus and the individual, where accepting Jesus Christ as one's personal Lord and savior becomes almost the whole of piety," to the extent that "if I'm all right with Jesus, then I don't need the church."[14] If I've been

---

[14] See Robert N. Bellah, "Religion and the Shape of National Culture," *America* 181/3 (1999) 12.

saved, justified through faith alone, have a personal relationship with Jesus and a "certainty of salvation," then I don't need to be engaged in the life of a Christian community, to worship with others, to be accountable to them, to be concerned for the common good and for a society that supports it.

From the time of Abraham, the People of God has been chosen in God's providence as a blessing for all the communities of the earth (Gen 12:3), a light to the nations (Isa 42:6; 49:6). God's salvation is mediated by God's people. To be a Jew meant to belong to the people of the covenant, Israel. So too being a disciple of Jesus means essentially being a member of his movement, his community, the church. This is where we come to know him, in his Body. Thus knowledge of God cannot be reduced to an interior enlightenment such as Gnostic movements in every age have promised, to a privatized piety, to my ideas about God, or to a concern for ethics, the perennial temptation of liberal theology. One cannot be a Christian all alone.

For all Paul's emphasis in Romans and Galatians that we are saved by faith, not by works of the Law, the ritual, communal, and what the later church would call sacramental dimensions of his understanding of God's grace in Christ are clear. His letters are always to or about churches. We are saved by our baptismal incorporation into the one body of Christ and by being given to drink of one Spirit (cf. 1 Cor 12:13). Baptism breaks down divisions between peoples, so that there is no longer Jew or Greek, slave or free, male or female (Gal 3:28; cf. 1 Cor 12:12). By our communion (*koinōnia*) in the body and blood of Christ we are united as his body for the world (cf. 1 Cor 10:16-18). The church has a ministry of reconciliation, a particular responsibility of its apostolic ministers (2 Cor 5:18). It is to be a sign or instrument of "communion with God and of the unity of the entire human race" (LG 1). Ratzinger sees this as the inner core of the concept of church. The church is *communio*; she is God's communing with humans and their communing with one another, and thus it is a sacrament or instrument of salvation. "The Church is the celebration of the Eucharist; the Eucharist is the Church."[15] That raises the question of the sacraments, which we will consider in the next chapter.

---

[15] Ratzinger, *Principles of Catholic Theology*, 53.

Chapter 12

"The communion of saints,
the forgiveness of sins"

In spite of its original use as a profession of faith made at baptism, the Apostles' Creed does not seem to say anything explicitly about the sacraments. Unlike the Nicene-Constantinopolitan Creed, it does not even mention baptism. Though some commentators see the phrase on the communion of saints (*sanctorum communionem*) as implying the church's sacramental structure, others interpret it as referring to the fellowship of all believers. The phrase did not appear in the earlier versions of the Creed which originated in Rome. But the final phrases of the Creed, communion of saints and forgiveness of sins, presume the church's sacramental life. We will explore the connection between communion, forgiveness, and the sacraments in this chapter.

Sanctorum Communionem

The Latin phrase, *sanctorum communionem*, most probably originated in Gaul. It first appears in a commentary by Nicetas of Remesiana (d. 414); Nicetas used it to describe the church as the fellowship of holy persons of all ages: "patriarchs, prophets, martyrs, and all other righteous men who have lived or are now alive, or shall live in time to come."[1] But the Latin

---

[1] J. N. D. Kelly, *Early Christian Creeds*, Third Edition (New York: Longman, 1972) 391.

phrase is ambiguous; it could mean the masculine "communion of holy people" or the neuter "communion of holy things." The latter meaning is how the Greek equivalent phrase, *koinōnia tōn hagiōn*, was understood in the East. The holy things were the eucharistic elements, a usage that still endures in the Orthodox liturgy when the deacon intones before the communion of the faithful, "Holy Things for God's Holy People." Without denying that the words were often taken in the West as referring to the sacrament, J. N. D. Kelly argues that the dominant conception there between the fifth and eighth centuries was of a "fellowship with holy persons."[2]

Still, Joseph Ratzinger is correct when he says that the phrase "refers first of all, to the eucharistic community, which through the Body of the Lord binds the Churches scattered all over the world into *one* Church."[3] First, both the Eastern and the Western churches were aware of the phrase's sacramental implications, an understanding that was explicit in the East. More fundamentally, the sacramental and eucharistic implications can be excluded only by ignoring Paul's theology of the church as the Body of Christ, for it is precisely baptism (1 Cor 12:13) and Eucharist (1 Cor 10:16-17) that unite Christians as one body in one Spirit.

The Concept of Communion

The concept of communion (*koinōnia/communio*) is a rich one in the New Testament. It describes first of all our participation in the life of Christ and therefore the communion or fellowship we enjoy with one another. Paul tells us that we have been called to *koinōnia* with Jesus Christ our Lord (1 Cor 1:9). Our communion takes place through our sharing in the gospel (Phil 1:5), in the faith (Phlm 6), in the sufferings of Christ (Phil 3:10; 2 Cor 1:7), in the Lord's Supper (1 Cor 10:16-17), and in his Spirit (2 Cor 13:13). The author of the second letter to Peter goes so far as to say that through God's promises "you may come to share [*koinōnoi*] in the divine nature" (2 Pet 1:4). There is a profoundly trinitarian dimension to our participation in the divine life, expressed by Paul in his benediction at the end of his second letter to the Corinthians: "The grace of the Lord Jesus Christ and the love of God and the fellowship of the holy Spirit be with all of you" (2 Cor 13:13; cf. Phil 2:1).

At the same time, because we share in the divine life we share a common life with one another; we live in that communion of disciples that

---

[2] Ibid., 394.

[3] Joseph Ratzinger, *Introduction to Christianity* (San Francisco: Ignatius Press, 2004) 334.

is the church. For Irenaeus of Lyons, "where the Church is, there is the Spirit of God; and where the Spirit of God is, there is the Church, and every kind of grace" (*Against the Heresies* 3.24.1). Just as our communion with God and with one another is mediated by visible signs, so too the communion of the church is expressed visibly. Paul's letters indicate his concern to keep his scattered churches in communion with one another. He visited them regularly, dispatched apostolic delegates (2 Cor 9:3), and sponsored collections for the poor in the church of Jerusalem (1 Cor 16:1-4; 2 Cor 8:2–9:14; Rom 15:25-29).

As new churches were founded in the post-New Testament period, they continued to be linked by a communion that was visibly expressed. Signs of communion included eucharistic hospitality, letters of communion between the bishops, similar letters provided for travelers identifying them as faithful Christians, and as early as the third century communion with Rome.[4] A practice preserved in the church to this day was having a new bishop ordained by at least three bishops, to indicate that this new bishop and his church were in the communion of the church. Another is the practice of the priest or bishop dropping a particle of the host into the chalice just before communion, a vestige of the ancient practice of the *fermentum*, the sending of a small piece of bread from the bishop's Eucharist to be consumed by his priests at their liturgies or by the bishop of a neighboring church as a sign of communion. This practice may well have originated at Rome; it is mentioned by Irenaeus (ca. 202) and was still in force in the early fifth century. Finally, having a priest who has been episcopally ordained preside at a local community's Eucharist is a sign of the communion between that community and the universal (catholic) church.

Just as communion was valued and expressed visibly, so also those whose conduct was judged injurious to the community were excluded from its communion. Paul ordered the church at Corinth to separate from their community a man living in incest (1 Cor 5:2; cf. Matt 18:15-18). Later this exclusion from the community was part of the discipline of canonical penance. Basil of Caesarea (d. 379) describes various penances for those guilty of serious sin such as murder, adultery, or fornication. They would stand outside the church confessing their sins and asking for prayers. For a sin like intentional murder, their penance might last

---

[4] See Ludwig Hertling, *Communio: Church and Papacy in Early Christianity* (Chicago: Loyola University Press, 1972) 23–36.

as long as twenty years before they were allowed to partake again in the Eucharist.[5] In the Eastern Church the term *akoinōnatos* for those so excluded from the *koinōnia* appears as early as Nicaea (325), while the Western Church since the year 400 has used the term excommunication for those excluded from the church's sacramental life.

Thus the communion of the church as one body in Christ is sacramentally grounded, because we are given to drink of the one Spirit in baptism (1 Cor 12:13), have a participation or communion (*koinōnia*) in the Body and Blood of Christ, and are united as one body (1 Cor 10:16-17). This ecclesial meaning of Eucharist was still strong in Aquinas.[6] But as fewer of the faithful in the second millennium received the Eucharist, more attention was given to reception of "Holy Communion" as an act of devotion. The ecclesial meaning of the Eucharist was largely forgotten. Some Protestant traditions have lost the practice of the regular celebration of the Eucharist. Even in the first half of the twentieth century, many Catholics did not communicate regularly, out of a sense of personal unworthiness. Children were told in school not to chew the host. Even after the Second Vatican Council, many Catholics understand receiving Holy Communion in terms of a personal union with Christ, without awareness of its ecclesial meaning.

The Communion of Saints

Today the doctrine of the communion of saints is understood by many to mean that the faithful on earth, that is, those living in communion with Christ, are in communion with the faithful of every age who have gone before them, whether canonized officially or not. This ancient belief can be found in Nicetas of Remesiana as we have seen, in Augustine (d. 430), and in Faustus of Riez (452).[7] It is expressed liturgically today in the Feast of All Saints (November 1). As the author of the letter to the Hebrews says, "we are surrounded by so great a cloud of witnesses" (Heb 12:1). While the Catholic practice of invoking the intercession of Mary and the saints is not usually understood by Protestant Christians, it is rooted in the doctrine of the communion of the saints. If they and we share in the life of God, then we are still in communion with them and can ask their intercession.

---

[5] *Epistle* 217, Can. 56–84.

[6] See *Commentary on John* 6.7.2; *Commentary on 1 Cor* 11:7.

[7] See Kelly, *Early Christian Creeds*, 388–392.

Those from less liturgical traditions have frequently interpreted the phrase "communion of saints" exclusively in terms of the *congregatio fidelium*, the congregation of the faithful. While not incorrect theologically, it neglects the full richness of the meaning of communion in the early church, particularly in Paul. For Paul our intimate communion in the divine life and with one another was "accomplished through Christ's salvific actions made sacramentally present in the community."[8] This sacramental, ecclesial meaning of the communion of saints comes to expression in a 1992 Letter of the Congregation for the Doctrine of the Faith, on the church as communion: "The Church is a *Communion of the saints*, to use a traditional expression that is found in the Latin versions of the Apostles' Creed from the end of the fourth century. The common visible sharing in the goods of salvation (*the holy things*), and especially in the Eucharist, is the source of the invisible communion among the sharers (*the saints*)."[9]

The Forgiveness of Sins

The church's sacramental life is also implicated in the phrase about the forgiveness of sins. While the New Testament proclaims the forgiveness of sins for those in the community of Jesus, that is, those who have been baptized, it also explicitly links forgiveness with baptism. Jesus instructed his disciples to proclaim the forgiveness of sins to those who would come after them, those who would be gathered in the church (Luke 24:47; John 20:23). On Pentecost Peter exhorts the people, "Repent and be baptized, every one of you, in the name of Jesus Christ for the forgiveness of your sins" (Acts 2:38). Ananias tells Paul after his conversion, "Get up and have yourself baptized and your sins washed away" (Acts 22:16). Paul says that we are baptized into Christ's death, so that we might live a new life in him, free from the power of sin and death (Rom 6:3-14; cf. 1 Cor 6:11; Col 2:12-13; Eph 5:26-27). In John's gospel, Jesus tells Nicodemus that "no one can enter the kingdom of God without being born of water and Spirit" (John 3:5).

It is difficult for many today to acknowledge our need for the forgiveness of sin. Joseph Ratzinger once wrote that "the spiritual crisis of our

---

[8] Michael A. Fahey, "Ecclesial Community as Communion," *The Jurist* 36 (1976) 17.

[9] CDF, "Letter to the Bishops of the Catholic Church on Some Aspects of the Church Understood as Communion," no. 6.

time has its basis in the obscuration of the grace of forgiveness."[10] The doctrine of original sin, first formulated by Augustine, has been virtually abandoned by many today. Yet the idea that each of us has been damaged by the sin so obviously present in the world, our cultures, our families, and our relationships, remains one of the great insights of the Christian tradition. Furthermore, few today acknowledge personal sin. We explain away our own cooperation in evil, blame it on parents or society, cherish our resentments, and psychologize our failings. Too often therapists have become our contemporary confessors, absolving not the sinner but the sin. The very word sin is rarely heard.

What then is the connection between baptism and forgiveness? In speaking of baptism we use the language of forgiveness, new life, grace, and the Holy Spirit, but what are the social and theological realities underlying the phenomenon of baptism that makes this language meaningful? What does it mean in terms of our experience?

From a biblical perspective, both sin and grace are social concepts, not just individual ones. In the Genesis story, the sin of our first parents affects not only themselves; rather, it lets sin loose as a destructive force in the world. When humans try to be their own gods (Gen 3:5), the harmony of God's creation is overturned. Thus the story of the fall in Genesis is immediately followed by a fratricide, Cain's murder of his brother Abel (Gen 4:1-16), and then by the great flood which nearly destroys creation (Gen 6:5–8:22). At the end of the Genesis pre-history comes the story of the confusing of language at Babel, isolating human beings from each other (Gen 11:1-9). In the imagery that lies behind this account of the creation, fall, and flood, the sin of Adam and Eve allows the waters of chaos, overcome by God's creative work, to rush back upon the earth with devastating effect, until God must intervene.

In his letter to the Romans, Paul also speaks of sin as a malevolent power which enters the world with Adam, bringing with it death. His classic formulation is "through one person sin entered the world, and through sin, death, and thus death came to all, inasmuch as all sinned" (Rom 5:12), not "in whom all have sinned," as it was mistranslated by Jerome in the Latin of the Vulgate.

But if sin is mediated socially, so too is grace. We say that baptism, the rite of initiation into the Christian community, means forgiveness, the

---

[10] Joseph Ratzinger, *Called to Communion: Understanding the Church Today* (San Francisco: Ignatius Press, 1996) 149.

remission of sins, the cleansing of original sin, and new life in the Spirit precisely because it brings the one baptized into a new community of people living, not in the spirit of "the world" (in the pejorative sense), but in the Holy Spirit of Jesus. In experiential terms it means, at least ideally, a radical change of social context. To be a member of a Christian community means to live where men and women gather in Christ's name, celebrate his presence in worship, proclaim his Gospel, follow his teachings, minister to others in his name, and live in his Spirit.

We know how important social context is. Each of us is formed and shaped, for better or worse, by a network of relationships—familial, social, and cultural. We recognize how seriously disadvantaged those children are who are neglected by their parents, experience physical or sexual abuse from family members or trusted friends (even members of the clergy as we have recently learned to our shame), or grow up in neighborhoods scarred by gang violence. We know how important it is for a child to grow up in a loving home, to be cherished by parents and siblings. We know how we are affected by the consumerism, secularism, and relativism of our culture, and we know how we are changed when we experience that we are loved. We feel a new energy, and new possibilities open up for us.

In a similar way, the Spirit present in the community called church mediates a new way of living based on the story of Jesus, his presence in word and sacrament, and life in his Spirit. The example of others living in Christ makes it possible for us to overcome sin. How can we know Jesus without the community of believers? That's why it makes little sense to baptize an infant whose parents are not practicing their faith; it does not mean necessarily that they are bad people, but that there is no church present in their home, no way that Jesus can be known or experienced. We are radically social beings. Relationships are real; we are formed by them.

Conclusion

The phrase, *communio sanctorum*, gives expression to the work of the Spirit, uniting us with the triune God and with one another. Placed after the third article of the Creed confessing our belief in the Holy Spirit, the phrase is both pneumatological and ecclesiological. It embraces those united by the Spirit into a communion, though from the beginning it was understood as extending beyond the present members of the church to embrace the prophets and saints of the first covenant as well as the saints and martyrs, living and dead. What God does for us in Christ, God as Spirit does in us as church.

While the first meaning of *koinōnia tōn hagiōn* in the East was the eucharistic elements, in the West the sacramental meaning was later and secondary. Still, it can be ignored only at the cost of Paul's vision of the role of baptism and the Eucharist in uniting believers into the one Body of Christ. Paul's theology here provides the grounds for what is today called a eucharistic ecclesiology such as one finds in the works of Pope Benedict.

> The Church is *communio*; she is God's communing with men in Christ and hence the communing of men with one another—and, in consequence, sacrament, sign, instrument of salvation. The Church is the celebration of the Eucharist; the Eucharist is the Church; they do not simply stand side by side; they are one and the same.[11]

To this day, Protestants prefer to translate *koinōnia* as "fellowship," while Catholics, more sensitive to its sacramental implications, generally prefer "communion."

Paul says, "the kingdom of God is not a matter of food and drink, but of righteousness, peace, and joy in the holy Spirit" (Rom 14:17). The church becomes "the initial budding forth of that kingdom" (LG 5).[12] How sad when the church fails to witness to that righteousness and peace it is its mission to proclaim.

---

[11] Joseph Ratzinger, *Principles of Catholic Theology: Building Stones for a Fundamental Theology* (San Francisco: Ignatius Press, 1987) 53.

[12] Translation from Walter M. Abbott, *The Documents of Vatican II* (New York: American Press, 1966).

Chapter 13

"The resurrection of the body, and the life everlasting, Amen."

Jesus' resurrection, his victory over the death that each of us must one day face, together with his sending of the Spirit, represents the climax or perfection of God's revelation: "He revealed that God was with us, to deliver us from the darkness of sin and death, and to raise us up to eternal life" (DV 4).

Today many have lost sight of this central doctrine, though its inclusion in the Apostles' Creed underlines its dogmatic status. Many Christians focus on the immortality of the soul rather than on the resurrection of the body, the legacy of Hellenistic philosophy on the formative centuries of Christianity. Some people today, influenced by Eastern philosophy or various New Age movements, appeal to the doctrine of reincarnation. Others remain ignorant of the basic Christian belief that we are created for an eternity in God's presence, to see God "face to face" (1 Cor 13:12). Both the immortality of the soul and the resurrection of the body express Christian hope in the promise of everlasting life. We will consider both concepts in this chapter.

Resurrection

The Catholic tradition is at its best when faith and reason work in harmony. The evidence for the immortality of the soul is primarily philosophical; it is the product of rational reflection, not revelation. An analysis of human knowing, the ability of intelligence to reach beyond the sensible, to reason abstractly, to raise questions about the infinite, the good, and the true, to grasp the virtually unconditioned—all this suggests that the human intellect is a spiritual power that cannot be reduced to the material.

The Congregation for the Doctrine of the Faith reaffirmed the church's belief in the immortality of the soul in a recent letter on eschatology: "The church affirms that a spiritual element survives and subsists after death, an element endowed with consciousness and will, so that the 'human self' subsists. To designate this element, the church uses the word 'soul,' the accepted term in the usage of scripture and tradition."[1] Still, Christian hope is rooted ultimately not in Greek philosophy but in the New Testament conviction in the resurrection of the body and life everlasting. As John Thiel writes, "If Jesus' afterlife is normative for the afterlife of believers, then the New Testament narratives insist on the indispensability of embodiment for identity."[2] We will be raised up in our bodies, in our full humanity.

The Resurrection of the Body

For most of the period reflected in the Old Testament, death was the end of life; there was no notion of a life beyond Sheol, the abode of the dead where relationship with Yahweh simply ceased (Ps 6:6; 88:6). It was only very late in Old Testament history, during the persecution under Antiochus IV (167–164 BCE) who sought to unite his kingdom by Hellenizing the Jews and outlawed the practice of their religion (1 Macc 1:10-63), that belief in a life beyond the grave began to take shape. With many choosing death rather than renounce their covenant relation with Yahweh, the hope that the God of the living might also be a God who could raise the dead to life entered the Jewish tradition (Dan 12:1-3; 2 Macc 7:9, 23; 12:43-46). The very late book of Wisdom, written in the last half of the first century BCE, seems to have been influenced by the Greek teaching on the soul: "the souls of the just are in the hand of God, and no torment shall touch them" (Wis 3:1). Thus belief in the resurrection of the dead was already present at the time of

---

[1] CDF, "Letter on Certain Questions Concerning Eschatology," *Origins* (August 2, 1979) 122.

[2] John E. Thiel, "For What May We Hope? Thoughts on the Eschatological Imagination," *Theological Studies* 67 (2006) 531.

Jesus in some segments of the Jewish community, particularly among the Pharisees (Mark 12:18-27).

That we are to share in the Resurrection is fundamental to the teaching of the New Testament. One finds it everywhere. The Synoptics represent Jesus as proclaiming the resurrection of the dead against the Sadducees, who rejected it (Mark 12:18-27; Matt 22:23-32; Luke 20:27-38). In John, Jesus says, "the hour is coming and is now here when the dead will hear the voice of the Son of God, and those who hear will live" (John 5:25). John's gospel refers only twice to the kingdom of God (John 3:3, 5), so central to Jesus' preaching in the Synoptics; instead the author refers frequently to eternal life, his deeper understanding of the mystery of salvation in light of the Resurrection. In his letter to the Romans, Paul argues that our baptism unites us to the death and resurrection of Jesus, so that his new life beyond death might become ours (Rom 6:3-6). While Paul's view of the Resurrection is radically christological, behind it lies the Jewish belief in the resurrection of the body.

Paul devoted a whole chapter to the resurrection of the body in his first letter to the church at Corinth (1 Cor 15). To our ears, his argument *from* the resurrection of the dead *to* the resurrection of Jesus sounds strange. But it makes perfect sense for one trained as a Pharisee. "But if Christ is preached as raised from the dead, how can some among you say there is no resurrection of the dead? If there is no resurrection of the dead, then neither has Christ been raised. And if Christ has not been raised, then empty [too] is our preaching; empty, too, your faith" (1 Cor 15:12-14). Paul speaks of Christ as the "firstfruits" of the Resurrection: "For just as in Adam all die, so too in Christ shall all be brought to life, but each one in proper order: Christ the firstfruits; then, at his coming, those who belong to Christ" (1 Cor 15:22-23; cf. v. 20).

Paul's usually clear language begins to falter when he tries to answer the question about what kind of body the dead will have (1 Cor 15:35). His contrast of a physical body with a spiritual body (*sōma pneumatikon*), that is to say, one characterized by spirit, is not terribly helpful (1 Cor 15:36-49). A spiritual body is really an oxymoron. Part of the difficulty is that we can understand what Paul is trying to say, but cannot really imagine it. For Paul, "body" (*sōma*) referred to the whole person, destined for immortality (1 Cor 15:45-53), thus a human being in his or her corporeal and social aspects. As opposed to *sōma*, flesh (*sarx*) refers to the carnal, sexual, and corruptible aspects of body. He compares the resurrection of the dead to a seed that is sown, dies, and gives forth new life

(1 Cor 15:36-44). Two points stand out; first, radical transformation, and second, some kind of continuity of identity.[3]

In one of his most substantive theological works, Joseph Ratzinger rejects the traditional view of belief in the immortality of the soul, based on a supposed Hellenic/Platonic dualism, as "something of a theologian's fantasy."[4] He argues that Plato did not develop a unified philosophy of the soul in relation to the body, that his doctrine of immortality was never purely philosophical, but in part religious, related to his concept of justice in the polis or civic community as that which leads to the integration of the person. In Aristotle, the soul is not immortal; as an organic principle or "entelechy" it remains bound to its matter as its form, and thus, is perishable. Although some of the mystery cults promised immortality, Ratzinger says that "the fundamental mood of antiquity at the time when Christianity was spreading could be described as stamped by despair."[5] Against this, he argues that the biblical pronouncements about the Resurrection mean not "a restoration of bodies to souls after a long interval" but that they live on "not by virtue of their own power, but because they are known and loved by God in such a way that they can no longer perish."[6]

In the Middle Ages there was much speculation about how the earth would give up its dead and the resurrection of the body would take place. Artists pictured the bodies of the dead rising from their tombs or being regurgitated by the animals or fish that had devoured them. Scholastics debated about whether fingernails and hair would be part of the risen body and tried to estimate the age at which the dead would be raised. They worried about the material continuity of the earthly body with the heavenly and wondered about how the bodies of those in hell would burn without being consumed. John Scotus Erigena (800–877) argued that just as Christ rose without biological sex, so would we, though this was contrary to the general view. Monastic writers used images of flowering and fertility to describe the risen body; some, especially the Cistercians, spoke of a double resurrection, of the soul as well as of the body, or of bodily immortality no longer subject to the corruption or

---

[3] See Caroline Walker Bynum, *The Resurrection of the Body in Western Christianity*, 200–1336 (New York: Columbia University Press, 1995) 6.

[4] Joseph Ratzinger, *Eschatology: Death and Eternal Life* (Washington, DC: The Catholic University of American Press, 1988) 145.

[5] Ibid., 142–45 at 145.

[6] Joseph Ratzinger, *Introduction to Christianity* (San Francisco: Ignatius Press, 2004) 353.

decay of the flesh. What lies behind these views catalogued at length by Caroline Walker Bynum are "the abstruse speculations of medieval theologians about what must be reassembled at the end of time to constitute a 'person.'"[7] Thus these theologians grasped the essential issue, but their speculative efforts show the futility of trying to imagine what can only be understood.

It was Thomas Aquinas in the thirteenth century who reinterpreted Aristotle by arguing that the soul was not just the spiritual "form" of the body, as Aristotle had taught, but also that it was personal, an intellectual substance that makes us human and opens us to immortality.[8] But Thomas was not really able to explain how the soul apart from the body was able to understand individual things, suggesting that perhaps God infused the species or ideas.[9]

Belief in the resurrection of the body means that God brings the whole person to life; it means that each of us hopes one day to come into God's presence as the person we have been and are, with our memory, our personality, and our relationships—most of all our relationship with God—all of which constitute the most important aspects of our personal identity.

Eternal Life

Eternal life is a corollary of the resurrection of the body but again, it is something we can better understand than imagine. The idea that each person must one day face God's judgment is everywhere in the New Testament. Paul says that "the wages of sin is death, but the gift of God is eternal life in Christ Jesus" (Rom 6:23; cf. 2:7). In the Gospel of John, Jesus speaks of many dwelling places in his Father's house, telling the disciples that he goes to prepare a place for them (John 14:2). The book of Revelation uses the image of the New Jerusalem coming down from heaven as the dwelling for the just (Rev 21:2-3). "Behold, God's dwelling is with the human race. He will dwell with them and they will be his people and God himself will always be with them [as their God]. He will wipe every tear from their eyes, and there shall be no more death or mourning, wailing or pain, [for] the old order has passed away" (Rev 21:3-4).

Heaven and hell, of course, are not places; they are modes of being. Heaven means to live in communion with God, to see God face to face,

---

[7] Bynum, *The Resurrection of the Body*, 342.

[8] Ratzinger, *Death and Immortality*, 148–49.

[9] ST I,89,4.

to be known, even as we are known (1 Cor 13:12). Thus John can say, "this is eternal life, that they should know you, the only true God, and the one whom you sent, Jesus Christ" (John 17:3).

What about those who die in their sins? Paul teaches us that the wicked cannot inherit the kingdom of God (1 Cor 6:10; Gal 5:19-21). Matthew and Revelation speak of eternal damnation as the destination of the wicked (Matt 25:41; Rev 20:10). John says that they will rise to "the resurrection of condemnation" (John 5:29). While the church has never said definitively that anyone is actually in hell, some argue that the existence of so much obvious evil demands that those who have excluded God from their lives are destined for the life they have chosen, without love, completely self-sufficient, without God. For one created for union with the divine, this is indeed hell.

A tradition in the Christianity of the East hopes that in the end all will be saved. Thérèse of Lisieux was supposed to have said, "I believe in hell but I think that it is empty." For Edward Schillebeeckx, such solutions seem to trivialize the drama of the conflict between good and evil that is so real. Instead, he argues that heaven and hell are "asymmetrical affirmations of faith." They are not on the same level. Those who live and die in communion with God look forward to a life with God that cannot be destroyed. For those who have resisted God's holiness, death is the end; there is no being raised to life, no kingdom of hell next to the joyful kingdom of God. "So there is no future for evil and oppression, while goodness still knows a future beyond the boundary of death, thanks to the outstretched hand of God which receives us. God does not take vengeance; he leaves evil to its own, limited logic."[10]

Conclusion

The Creed's emphasis on the resurrection of the dead (or of the flesh, in its earliest versions) was a clear repudiation of the Gnostic teaching that the material world was evil. Christianity teaches that creation is good (Gen 1:1–2:4a), the work of God's hands (Ps 8:7; 102:26). Paul suggests that "creation itself," sharing in Christ's gift of the Spirit, "would be set free from its slavery to corruption and share in the glorious freedom of the children of God" (Rom 8:20).

---

[10] Edward Schillebeeckx, *Church: The Human Story of God* (New York: Crossroad, 1990) 138.

As Christianity moved out of its original home in the thought world of Judaism and into a very different world, informed by Greco-Roman culture, it was not able to entirely free itself of the dualism of Greek thought. Both the Greek mystery religions and Gnosticism recognized personal immortality. But for both, it was the immortality of the soul. The body belonged to the world of corruptibility and change; it had no destiny beyond the grave. There are traces of this dualism today in much of our Christian spirituality that privileges the spiritual and is suspicious of the physical, the embodied, especially the sexual. The emphasis on sexual renunciation in the early church had the effect, in the words of Peter Brown, of tending "to prise the human person loose from the physical world."[11]

But from its earliest days Christianity taught the doctrine of the resurrection of the body and everlasting life. Therefore, respect for the body was important; a "temple of the holy Spirit," it was destined for resurrection (cf. 1 Cor 6:13-19). In confessing the resurrection of the body and life everlasting, the Apostles' Creed challenged the dominant culture of its time, just as it continues to challenge our own.

Paul sees the Resurrection not merely as a new form of personal life but as our being taken up into the divine life of God who is Father, Son, and Spirit: "If the Spirit of the one who raised Jesus from the dead dwells in you, the one who raised Christ from the dead will give life to your mortal bodies also, through his Spirit that dwells in you" (Rom 8:11). If our bodies are destined for immortality, then our embodied relationships take on new value. Our sexuality, our relations with family and friends, with the poor, are constitutive of who we are and what we will become. Our embodied relationships thus reveal our relationship to the author of all life and communion.

The Preface for the Mass of Christian Burial expresses beautifully this hope of those who die in the Lord: "Lord for your faithful people life is changed, not ended. When the body of our earthly dwelling lies in death we gain a new and everlasting dwelling place in heaven."

[11] Peter Brown, *The Body and Society: Men, Women and Sexual Renunciation in Early Christianity* (New York: Columbia University Press, 1988) 432.

Postscript

The mystery at the heart of the Christian faith that we confess in the Apostles' Creed is the one God who is called Father, Son, and Holy Spirit. This trinitarian language, the result of considerable controversy in the early church, as we have seen, can be easily misunderstood. As we draw this work to a close we need to reflect once more on *what* we are affirming with our God language. Finally, and most importantly, we need to try to express *how* we experience within us this divine mystery as Father, Son, and Spirit.

Describing the Triune God

The Creed's references to Father, Son, and Spirit in terms of their works of creation, redemption, and sanctification can give the false impression of a chronology in which each work follows the other as different acts, operations, or episodes. As Nicholas Lash says, "Insofar as the scheme of one drama with three acts is allowed to shape the sense of our relationship to Father, Son, and Spirit, it draws us back towards some version of the oldest of all families of trinitarian heresy, known as 'modalism,'" a heresy which reduces differentiations within the Godhead to different modes of working or appearing.[1] In more popular language, it makes the Fall the reason for the Incarnation, reducing God's self-disclosure in Christ to an afterthought, something caused by human sin.

We thus illegitimately divide up the work of the one God, so that the Father creates, the Son redeems, the Spirit sanctifies. We also tend to

---

[1] Nicholas Lash, *Believing Three Ways in One God: A Reading of the Apostles' Creed* (Notre Dame, IN: University of Notre Dame Press, 1993) 30.

insert the divine work within a temporal framework—as though it took place in time—so that creation becomes a work of the past, the redemption a transaction at a moment in history, and salvation something yet to come. There is a necessary asymmetry between the temporal categories in which we think and the effort we must make to see God's work from a perspective "outside" of time. Thus, it makes more sense to see creation as ongoing, nature always graced as well as damaged by sin, and the Spirit's work as incorporating us into the mystery of Christ's living, dying, and rising, thus gathering us into God's life flowering in us today as well as in the future. Irenaeus of Lyons (ca. 180) spoke of God's creating and redeeming through his "hands," the Son and the Spirit,[2] emphasizing that God as Father, Son, and Spirit is involved in both works. In more technical trinitarian language, theologians have used the Greek word *perichorēsis,* a mutual indwelling of the divine persons in one another.

Still, if the divine work of creation, redemption, and sanctification involves all three persons, and thus is inseparable, Aquinas makes a distinction in regard to the Incarnation between a divine action *"ad extra"* and the "term" or realization in space and time of that action, which more properly belongs to a person. In the words of Gerald O'Collins:

> Only the son assumes a human existence and actualizes—or rather is—the personal being of Jesus. As regards the first person of the Trinity, only the Father eternally generates the Son, a life-giving act *ad intra* that finds its parallel in the Father raising the dead Jesus . . . The term of that action *ad extra* is also specific and distinct: the new, glorified life of Jesus, who with the Father sends the Spirit into the world.[3]

The fact that the church's trinitarian language adopted the word person (Greek: *prosōpon;* Latin: *persona*) has also caused some misunderstandings. Many have confused the language of three persons in one God as meaning that God is three persons in the modern psychological sense, three selves or independent centers of understanding, willing, and acting. They seem to think of God as three people, thus coming dangerously close to a tritheism.

---

[2] *Adversus Haereses* V,1,3; V,28,4.

[3] Gerald O'Collins, *The Tripersonal God: Understanding and Interpreting the Trinity* (New York: Paulist Press, 1999) 181; cf. Aquinas, *Summa Theologica* 3a.3.1-4.

Some theologians today prefer to avoid the word person, speaking instead of "three modes of being" (Barth) or three "distinct manners of subsisting" (Rahner). Others maintain that the modern sense of person has something to help illumine trinitarian theology, not the least that it is personal, stressing the importance of relationships. Gerald O'Collins is less comfortable with theologizing on the basis of the modern concept of the person. Still, he says that in the Trinity one consciousness subsists in a threefold way, shared by all three persons, "mutually distinct only in and through their relations of origins."[4] The Father is unoriginate, the Son is generated eternally by the Father, and the Spirit proceeds from the Father through the Son. The Son is aware that he is not the Father, and the Spirit is aware of being distinct from the Father and the Son, but their knowing, willing, and acting are identical.

Michael Downey speaks of the doctrine of the Trinity as a grammar, that like all grammars, provides rules or parameters within which the truth may be sought. The grammar of the Trinity enables us to speak about the mystery of the self-giving God who is Love. "The term 'person' when used of God is a way of saying that God is always toward and for the other in the self-giving which is constitutive of love. Self-giving is always in relation to another, to others."[5]

Thus relationality is at the very heart of the Christian understanding of God. So too the human person, by nature open to the other, finds meaning, happiness, and fulfillment only in relationships with others and the Other who is God. We are called to communion with God who is Father, Son, and Spirit. That communion is real; the transcendent God is also immanent. The divine mystery discloses itself within us. Thus we need to ask, however tentatively, how do we experience God as Father, Son, and Spirit?

Experiencing the Triune God

The Father speaks in silence. We sense God's presence, quiet, reassuring, beyond image and word. We know that we have been touched, that we are not alone. The Father's presence is comforting, sustaining, and life-giving. It brings a deep sense of peace. But the very taste of God awakens a deeper hunger, a desire for more, for some way to move beyond the veil, to see God's face.

---

[4] O'Collins, *The Tripersonal God*, 178.

[5] Michael Downey, *Altogether Gift: A Trinitarian Spirituality* (Maryknoll, NY: Orbis Books, 2000) 48–55 at 54.

The created world, especially nature, reflects the majesty of its creator. The blue of the afternoon sky draws us up and out of ourselves and into its vastness. We feel God's comforting touch in the warmth of the sun or the freshness of the rain. We taste God's sweetness in the rich smell of the earth. We rejoice in the exuberance and variety of God's creatures bursting with life, from the sparrow chirping outside our window to the tiny baby who clings so tightly to our finger. We experience God's love in the touch of a friend. The nighttime canopy of stars suggests a presence that is mysterious and yet near.

The Son's presence is more challenging. He has a voice. We know him from the gospels, we have seen him with his disciples, and we strive to make his words our own. His words are not always comforting. He calls us to conversion and to service, inviting us to follow him. He tells us we must lose our life to save it, that the last shall be first, that we must carry our cross with him, that we can embrace him in the poor.

We experience Jesus as "Lord." He has a claim on us, and we on him. The relation is mutual and personal. We ask for strength, for mercy, for forgiveness, and sense that he has taken away our sin, that in him we have been pardoned and set free. Thus to be "in Christ" is to be a "new creation" (2 Cor 5:17).

Christ also has a body, both sacramental and ecclesial. What is most intimate for Catholics is perhaps also most difficult to express, their sense that the risen Jesus comes to them personally in the Eucharist, that they have a communion in his Body and Blood. At the same time, in our communion with Christ we sense also our communion with one another in his Body which is the church.

The Spirit is not itself an object of our consciousness; we recognize its presence reflexively in our interior lives. We "discern" the Spirit's presence. The Spirit inspires, animates, and breathes within us. The Spirit is the living source of our faith. We find that even in our doubts, we are convinced that God is real, that we are able to call on God as *Abba* (Rom 8:15), confess Jesus as Lord (1 Cor 12:3), and know that our sins have been forgiven (Rom 6:20-23). We experience the "fruit of the Spirit [in] love, joy, peace, patience, kindness, generosity, faithfulness, gentleness, self-control" (Gal 5:22-23).

We recognize the Spirit's presence in the movements of our hearts, in our affectivity. We feel it in gratitude, a song of joy that wells up within. We recognize it in the sorrow and sense of forgiveness that heals our wounds. An interior freedom (2 Cor 3:17; Gal 5:1) that enables us to be our best selves, to discover who we truly are is evidence of the Spirit's presence. We are drawn by the Spirit in love, the greatest of the Spirit's gifts (1 Cor 13:13), towards the God we cannot see and to find within ourselves a compassion for others that is not our own. Thus we experience the work of the triune God within us. This is the Christian mystery that is confessed in the Apostles' Creed.

Index

In the spirit of nineteenth-century philosopher John Stuart Mill's admonition to "fully, frequently, and fearlessly" discuss what we profess to be true in order that it remain a "living truth" rather than "dead dogma," Thomas P. Rausch gives us *I Believe in God: A Reflection on the Apostles' Creed*. Rausch carefully explores the controversies that led to the development of the Creed and thereby brings the Creed to life for modern readers. More important, he maintains that the Creed is most fully alive when those who profess it do so as a personal response to their baptismal call.

I Believe in God carefully unpacks the three articles of the Creed but does so always with an eye and heart toward communion with God as Father, Son, and Holy Spirit. As baptized Christians, to profess the Creed is to be committed to enter more deeply into this trinitarian relationship and thus more fully into communion with one another. Rausch clearly shows that the Apostles' Creed is grounded in Scripture, first came to expression in the church's baptismal liturgy, and can be better understood in light of contemporary theological reflection. Attentive to the ways in which the language of the Creed is relevant to the experience of twenty-first-century Christians, he leads us to understand what Pope Benedict meant when he said the Creed is "a tiny *summa* in which everything essential is expressed." With Rausch's guidance, readers will confess those essentials with greater conviction and appreciation.

Thomas P. Rausch, SJ, is the T. Marie Chilton Professor of Catholic Theology at Loyola Marymount University in Los Angeles. He is the author of *Being Catholic in a Culture of Choice, Towards a Truly Catholic Church, Who Is Jesus?, Catholicism in the Third Millennium,* and editor of the bestselling *The College Student's Introduction to Theology,* all published by Liturgical Press.